FORD CAPRI

HIGH PERFORMANCE MODELS 1969-1987

FORD CAPRI

HIGH PERFORMANCE MODELS 1969-1987

◆

ESSENTIAL
ADVICE & DATA
FOR
BUYERS & ENTHUSIASTS

◆

Chris Horton

Windrow & Greene Automotive

Published in Great Britain by
Windrow & Greene Ltd
5 Gerrard Street
London W1V 7LJ

A CIP catalogue record for this book is available from the British Library.

ISBN 1 872004 02 4

Design: *ghk* DESIGN, Chiswick, London

Printed in Singapore

Contents

Part of the £22 million Ford spent developing the Capri went into modernising the assembly plants at Cologne in Germany and Halewood, just outside Liverpool. This view of Halewood dates from the 1980s but gives some idea of the scale of the company's investment over the years. The Capri was only ever assembled in any volume at these two plants and all production was transferred to Cologne in 1984.

ACKNOWLEDGEMENTS

I would like to thank John Hill of the Capri Club International for his enthusiastic help in providing both a huge number of cars to illustrate the Capri's main problem areas and an equally large number of historical photos from the club's extensive archives.

Thanks, too, to RS3100 owner Andy Smith and my good friend and 2.8 Injection owner Dave Sully for sharing their experiences of Capri ownership and making their cars available for photography — and to Peter Robain for shooting the front cover picture.

Last, but by no means least, thanks to my publisher, Bryan Kennedy, for wading through the text and keeping it within manageable proportions. It can't have been easy!

Chris Horton

Thame, Oxfordshire, January 1992

THE AUTHOR

Chris Horton has been a full-time motoring journalist since joining the staff of *Car Mechanics* in 1978. After editing *Kit Cars and Specials* from 1981 to 1982, he worked on *Sports Car Mechanics* and then *Classic Car Mechanics*, taking over as editor of the latter in 1986.

The magazine was later renamed *Restoring Classic Cars* and then *Your Classic*, and it is as Editor-at-Large of the latter that he currently earns his living. He has contributed to many other motoring magazines, both in the UK and abroad. Aged 35, he lives in Oxfordshire with his family, five classic Rover saloons and four cats.

1. Background and assessment

Even for a car manufacturer with the resources of the Ford Motor Company, the Capri was a remarkable achievement. It was in continuous production for the 18 years from November 1968 until December 1986 (and on sale from January 1969 until as recently as the autumn of 1987), and sales amounted to nearly two million. The first million were sold in less than five years.

That would have been creditable for a run-of-the-mill four-door family saloon; but the Capri, though undeniably practical when you got to know it, was also an unashamedly sporty-looking fastback. It certainly wasn't what Mr Average and his family were used to in the late 1960s.

It was thus a car which buyers would have to be convinced they really could justify owning, rather than one which, like the best-selling Cortina before it, they would flock to buy as a legitimate appliance for the mundane business of getting from A to B. It may well have been, according to Ford's oft-quoted slogan, 'the car you always promised yourself', but people would have to be prepared to put that promise into practice.

Not that Ford of Britain went too far out on a limb when, in July 1966, a management meeting gave the so-called Colt project its blessing. In the USA, Ford vice-president Lee Iacocca had exploited the tried-and-tested mechanical components of the company's Falcon saloon (and the earlier success of the Thunderbird 'personal' car) to create the enormously popular Mustang.

There seemed no reason at all, argued the management at Dearborn, even given the vastly different car-buying habits prevailing on this side of the Atlantic, why the same basic formula shouldn't be repeated all over again. (The Colt name was subsequently dropped for various reasons, not least because it had already been registered by the Japanese Mitsubishi company.)

In the event, the Capri was a joint Anglo-German effort rather than a purely British one. Even by the early 1960s it was becoming increasingly clear to Ford that the cost of developing new models would have to be spread over a far wider base, and equally clear that only a truly pan-European marketplace could generate the huge volume of sales required to provide a realistic return on its investment.

It was estimated that the Capri would cost £20 million to put into production; in the event, it cost £22 million. And there was already a precedent for this European co-operation. The Escort, due for release in 1968, was being designed and built by Ford's British and German operations, as had been, of course, the 1966-launched Transit van.

Just as Lee Iacocca in America had cleverly given the Mustang a unique selling point — it was a good-looking but essentially ordinary car which could be simply and economically tailored to the customer's needs with an enormous range of options and accessories — so the Capri offered a combination of features which few of its competitors could muster. It had four seats, for a start, and even if rear-seat headroom was necessarily restricted, two adults could still travel quite comfortably in the back for moderate distances.

The boot, even if it was fairly small and had to wait until 1974 to gain the versatility of a hatchback-type tailgate, could accept a reasonable

The very first Ford Capri bore little resemblance to the car which is the real subject of this book. Launched in 1961 as a development of the four-door Classic saloon, it sold less than 19,000 examples and is one of the least successful cars ever built by Ford of Britain.

The success of the Mustang in the USA convinced Ford that there was a market for a European equivalent. The 2+2 fastback, launched in 1964, proved a remarkably accurate foretaste of things to come from Halewood and Cologne.

amount of luggage; and it would have been a harsh critic indeed who could have found much to dislike about the car's sleek styling.

And, for a car which seemed so blatantly exotic, the Capri was remarkably practical. It looked as if there should have been a complex quad-cam V12 thrashing away under the bonnet, or a twin-cam straight-six at the very least. Instead, a simple overhead-valve four-cylinder engine drove the rear wheels through a four-speed manual gearbox to give near-100mph performance and excellent fuel economy from even the most basic model.

Straightforward but effective suspension gave it sure-footed but exhilarating road manners and a ride quality almost as good as any mid-range saloon; and what could sometimes seem a dauntingly wide range of trim and accessory options convinced would-be owners that, unlike every other British Ford to date, here was anything but a car for the masses. The irony of it was, of course, that the masses flocked to buy it.

The Capri offered exceptional value for money. Its nearest competitors, at the time of its launch, were the MGB GT and MGC GT, the fastback Sunbeam Rapier and, perhaps most interestingly, the then brand-new Reliant Scimitar GTE. All offered similar (and in the case of the Reliant better) performance and roadholding, but most were appreciably more expensive — if not in terms of initial purchase price alone, then in what Ford itself would later call 'cost of ownership'.

The 99mph Capri 1600GT, for example, cost £1,041 when it was launched. The MGB GT, on the other hand, even if it was slightly faster and cost only another £21, was still no more than a two-seater with room in the back for a couple of very small children. The Holbay-tuned 1725cc Sunbeam Rapier H120 offered much the same accommodation as the Ford, but was much dearer (£1,323), only two mph faster and, in practice, had little appeal to anyone but a long-time enthusiast of the Rootes Group.

Only the £1,759 Scimitar GTE came anywhere near providing the performance and interior accommodation of the £1,400 Capri 3000GT. It used the same V6 engine and pre-dated the first truly high-performance Capri by some four months; but the Reliant's inherently rather specialist nature

It was clear from the start that the Capri would have to be a joint Anglo-German effort and sold throughout Europe. To ensure that it could cope with the continent's widely differing climatic conditions, pre-production cars underwent rigorous weather-testing. Note the so-called knife-blade rear side windows of this example, only abandoned in favour of the familiar 'D'-shaped panes at a very late stage in the car's development.

always denied it the vital mass-market appeal of the Ford.

In the early 1970s the Capri reigned supreme in its class. Its best year was 1970 itself (238,913 sold), and although 1971 and 1972 were less encouraging, in 1973 sales climbed to an impressive 233,325. A series of mechanical revisions and a major body redesign (the 1974 hatchback Capri II) kept the car looking surprisingly fresh, even against increasing opposition from cars like the Datsun Z series. And, right from the start, success in most forms of motorsport had guaranteed the Capri a place in the heart and mind of anyone who took his driving seriously. (There was even a four-wheel-drive rallycross version which, although nowhere near as successful, pre-dated Audi's all-conquering quattro by nearly 15 years.)

By the end of the 1970s, however, the Capri was beginning to date. Despite Ford's effusive claims at its 1978 launch of the so-called Capri lll, this new model provided little more than further mechanical revisions and refinements in a marginally crisper body shell, and by the early 1980s increasing numbers of front-wheel-drive hatchbacks were making serious inroads into Capri sales. By 1980 annual sales had dropped to only 41,755.

Ford itself hammered a crucial nail into the Capri's coffin with the 1981 launch of the trend-setting Escort XR3, and by 1982 UK sales had dropped to less than 20,000.

In a way, though, the 1980s were the Capri's most interesting years, at least as far as performance-orientated British enthusiasts were concerned. Special editions based on four-cylinder Capris between 1982 and 1986 (Calypso, Cabaret, Cameo, Laser) were little more than marketing strategies to bolster up sales of an increasingly outmoded car, yet at the same time the 2.8 Injection captured the imagination of the car-buying public like no other Ford before or since.

Launched in June 1981 at around £8,000, the 2.8 Injection easily undercut the rather fragile Alfa Romeo GTV6 (£10,250) and even the increasingly overweight Datsun 280ZX (£8,641) and, by the time the final bells-and-whistles, buy-now-while-stocks-last Capri 280 had been sold late in 1987, no less than 25,000 had been built. What is rather more interesting about that bald statistic, though, is the fact that of those 25,000 2.8s, some 80 per cent were sold in Britain alone.

Indeed, of total Capri sales in 1983 of 27,618, over 22,000 were in Britain, so it was no small wonder that left-hand-drive production finally ceased at the end of 1984 — or that, despite the howls of protest from both enthusiasts and the press, the Capri eventually had to die. It had had a good run for its money, but Ford and the world simply had to move on. One wonders whether, in twenty years' time, there will be as much fuss over the Sierra Cosworth, the XR3-based RS Turbo or even the RS200.

This book sets out to guide the prospective purchaser of what has become since its demise a genuinely worthwhile classic car and to tell him (or

Only the glassfibre-bodied Reliant Scimitar GTE — which employed Ford's own 3.0-litre V6 engine nearly six months before Ford itself — was a serious threat to Capri sales. But it was more expensive and too specialised to detract from the phenomenal success of the Ford during the early 1970s.

her) not only what goes wrong with it, but also how to choose and then identify the best car for his needs in the first place.

Neither has the writer fallen into the trap — he hopes — of automatically assuming that all Capris are classics just because one or two of them have achieved that exalted status. In this case, the word 'classic' effectively means 'high performance', and advice is restricted to models capable of at least 100mph.

That still leaves an initially bewildering variety to choose from, particularly if one includes the German-market models like the 1700GT or V6-engined 2300GT, and the limited-production homologation specials like the RS2600 and RS3100. There are no less than five different engine types, too, available in something like 16 different capacities between them.

It's worth wading through this confusing nomenclature, however, and then buying the best example you can possibly find. Probably no car offers the same investment potential as money in a bank or building society, yet a well-chosen Capri, perhaps restored over the years but certainly used and maintained, will provide not only a reasonable return on your investment but an economical, practical and enjoyable means of transport as well.

The Capri's simple construction means that

remarkably little ever goes wrong with it — apart, that is, from the corrosion endemic in any unitary-construction steel body. Even the most exotic RS models are generally no more difficult or expensive to restore and maintain than the most basic 1600GT; and, perhaps most significantly, the Capri not only offers excellent value for money to buy in the first place but it's also extremely cheap to run. Parts and service are still widely available from Ford dealers throughout Europe — and possibly the world — and, in Britain at least, nearly every town has its resident Ford specialist.

This chapter must conclude with a few words of warning. Don't expect to make a financial killing on a Capri: enjoy it simply as a motor car, not as some priceless art treasure. Secondly, keep your wits about you when viewing prospective purchases. In the heat of the moment, it is easy to abandon your critical faculties and throw caution to the wind. A Capri, like any other collection of disparate components travelling in formation, can conceal mechanical and structural faults unless you know exactly what you are looking for.

Those faults are what we shall be looking at in Chapter Two, but don't be afraid to seek guidance elsewhere, if you feel you need it. The owners' clubs (addresses in Chapter Five) should be able to locate an enthusiastic owner in your area who's willing to share his experience, and there's no doubt that the moderating influence of a companion, knowledgeable or not, can save considerable heartache later on.

Finally, look at as many cars as you can and, unless you enjoy restoration as an end in itself, don't buy a basket-case with over-ambitious ideas of 'doing it up' and making a fast buck. Few classic cars are ever worth more than the sum of their component parts, never mind the time and effort required for a rebuild to a high standard. Better to buy a sound original specimen, or a well-restored one, in the first place.

At the time of writing, for example (late 1991), even a MkI 2000GT fit only for ground-up restoration will cost at least £750. You could probably buy a really good one for £2,000, and that first car will invariably cost three or four times more than the £1,250 difference to restore to the same standard.

THE FIRST CAPRI

The subject of this book was by no means the first Ford car to bear the name of the Italian island in the Mediterranean just off Naples, although it was certainly the most successful.

During the late 1950s, Ford of Britain was developing a mid-range family saloon to sell alongside the 105E Anglia. The result was a car which shared much of the Anglia's mechanical hardware — and, of course, its famous reverse-sloping rear window.

It was from this four-door saloon, launched in July 1961 and correctly (if somewhat clumsily) known as the Consul Classic 315, that the first Capri was developed and launched at the end of the same year.

Designed by Colin Neal — who today works as a stylist for Chrysler in the USA — the Classic Capri was mechanically identical to the Classic saloon, but visually immediately distinguished from it by its far more elegant tear-drop roof line.

Power was initially provided by the Classic's 1340cc Kent engine with a three-bearing crankshaft. It was replaced by a similar 1498cc five-bearing unit in July 1962, and this remained the standard power unit until both the Classic and Capri were discontinued in July 1964.

The Classic Capri GT was launched in February 1963. Again this used the five-bearing 1498cc engine, but it had a higher compression ratio, better manifolding and twin Weber carburettors to produce slightly more power.

In all, some 111,225 Classic saloons and 18,716 Classic Capris were built, and both cars still hold the dubious distinction of completing Ford of Britain's shortest production run to date — a far cry from the success of the subject of this book, and what to many people is the only 'real' Capri.

Both the Cologne and Halewood factories were kept busy during the late 1960s and early 1970s. In 1970 nearly 239,000 Capris of all types were sold, and although sales fell during 1971 and 1972 they climbed back to over 233,000 for 1973. (Capri Club International)

An impressive list of competition successes gave the Capri the right kind of image throughout
its 18-year life. It notched up numerous wins in both British and other European circuit events,
and in 1971 the four-wheel-drive rallycross cars were a popular spectacle.

WHICH IS WHICH?

The cars covered by this book have been selected, as we said earlier, on the grounds that they are — or certainly were when they were new — all capable of at least 100mph.

That eliminates all the 1300s and most of the 1600s, but we've deliberately retained the MkI 1600GT for its rarity and interest value. (With a top speed of 99mph it's close enough to make no difference.)

It's not easy to categorise the Capri range in any truly logical manner. Basically, though, it can be divided into UK-market cars, German-market cars (effectively sold throughout Ford's mainland European territories) and, finally, US-specification vehicles sold there between 1970 and 1977.

British-specification MkI Capris featured in-line four-cylinder Kent engines of either 1300 or 1600cc (all capacities are nominal figures), a 2.0-litre V4 or the so-called Essex 3.0-litre V6.

In Germany the MkI used 1300, 1500 or 1700 V4s (similar, but not identical, to the British V4), as well as 2000, 2300 and 2600 V6s. Of these V4-engined cars, only the 1700 was consistently capable of a genuine 100mph (162 km/h).

In Britain the 1600 Kent was replaced by the single-overhead-camshaft Pinto engine of the same nominal capacity in September 1973. The 2.0-litre V4 was dropped at the end of MkI production.

British-market MkIIs were still available with the 1300 Kent unit, however, plus the 2.0-litre Pinto (which effectively became the definitive Capri engine) and the 3.0-litre Essex V6.

At the same time, the German engine range was more or less standardised with the British one, with the notable exception of the 2.0-litre Pinto. In Germany and the rest of Europe, just to be awkward, the only engine between the 1600 Pinto and the 3.0-litre V6 was a 2300 V6.

The MkIII featured much the same range of engines as the MkII, both in Britain and Germany, although in 1981 the Essex V6 was replaced in both markets by the all-new (and substantially different) Cologne-designed V6 of 2.8 litres.

The Capri was exported to the USA (and sold through Ford's Lincoln-Mercury dealers) from April 1970, initially with the 1600 crossflow engine or the 2.0-litre overhead-cam Pinto. A 2.3-litre Pinto followed for this market alone, and V6-engined cars used either the German-built 2.6 or 2.8.

A full list of models and engines appears in Chapter Three, with mechanical specifications and performance figures of the most widely available high-performance Capris in Chapter Four.

Above: The Capri range might seem dauntingly wide at first sight, but it is actually quite straightforward to differentiate between Capris I, II and III. The Mk I was built from the car's introduction until December 1973, although post-September 1972 cars (the so-called facelift models) featured a number of modifications, not least the larger rear light units.

Below: The Capri II was introduced in February 1974, its most obvious distinguishing features being an opening tailgate and a much sleeker, smoother body.

Then in March 1978 came the Capri III — mechanically virtually identical to the earlier car but with numerous detail improvements and the easily recognised 'eyebrows' over the headlamps.

BEST BUYS

Suggesting a best buy from the range of Capris available is not easy. Much depends on individual preference, requirements — and not least your budget.

In very general terms, though, the best Capri you can buy will almost always be the one in the best structural and mechanical condition within a given price range. Restoring a rough example will invariably cost more than buying a similar model in sound condition, and even if you may be pushing your resources to their limit there's a strong case for spending a little more than you might have anticipated to get a sound example to start with.

A cheap, rough example will soon soak up any savings you might have earmarked for its improvement. And if you really can't afford to buy a sound example, at least try to find one with mechanical problems rather than rampant body corrosion. That's not to suggest that you won't spend a considerable sum of money overhauling worn-out engines, gearboxes and suspension systems, but you'll make better and quicker progress than if you try to rebuild a car with a terminally rotten body.

If you have the choice, go for a sound original car rather than one which has obviously been restored or renovated. Not only will it be worth more in the long run, but with a little care and attention it will probably last a lot longer, too. Restoration standards vary widely, from excellent to appalling, and by buying a car which has clearly had major mechanical and/or structural surgery at some time in its life you could be burdening yourself with someone else's insurmountable problems.

Decide, too, exactly why you need the car. If it is simply a Capri — any Capri — which you're after for practical everyday transport, then go for a simple 1.6- or 2.0-litre, ideally a MkII or III with the added versatility of a hatchback and easily obtainable spares. Both offer reasonable performance and handling and, as we shall explain in Chapter Six, can be uprated and tuned quite easily.

The performance-orientated V6-engined cars are more specialised and more expensive to buy and run, and we'd certainly urge you not to buy an exotic like an RS3100 unless you really want the responsibility of looking after it. A 3000E or GT will be just as much fun in practical, day-to-day terms.

The author's favourites, for what it's worth, are the MkII or III 2.0S, the V4-engined MkI 2000GT, and the MkI 30000E — although not necessarily in that order. Of the later cars, the 2.8 Injection is a very pleasant machine, albeit with a reputation perhaps a shade larger than life (go for the very slightly faster — and cheaper — four-speed cars rather than the later five-speeders) and don't be too concerned if you can't find or afford a Tickford or Zakspeed Turbo.

The former remains one of the most breathtakingly exciting rear-wheel-drive cars the author has driven, but it is inevitably more difficult and expensive to maintain and repair than a run-of-the-mill 2.8 or 3000, and it will almost certainly have been driven within an inch of its life at some time or other. High-profile cars like these tend to be rather more stealable, too...

Finally, don't bother paying over the odds for one of the last Brooklands Green 280s. They are extremely nice cars and they will always be highly collectable, but at the end of the day it will almost certainly be a sound MkI — and the earlier the better — which is the real prize. The sad fact is that it may already be too late to find one.

2. What to look for

Today's Capri buyer faces not only the normal problems to be expected when looking for an ageing classic car, but also, ironically, one or two major obstacles more likely in a vehicle four or five times its age and built in much smaller quantities. Body corrosion and mechanical failures are about average in terms of incidence and severity — more on both these later — but originality, if that is your goal, can be a real headache.

The confusingly wide variety of paint, trim and accessory options — well over 900 according to some authorities — means that relatively few spares of each type will have been made in the first place, and because of storage problems, most dealers will have discarded remaining stocks long ago. You can gauge some idea of the scale of the problem from the section on chassis and trim identification plates at the end of Chapter Four.

Added to this is the fact that early cars — by which we mean pre-1974 MkIs — are now so rare, either for spares, repair or (particularly) in sound original condition, that to all intents and purposes it's the later MkIIs and IIIs that we'll have to concentrate on here. (These do constitute the bulk of the real high performers, in any case.)

MkIs *can* still be found, albeit in rapidly diminishing numbers. But unless they are near-perfect in every detail (or as rare and historically significant as Andy Smith's RS3100 featured in Chapter Seven) they will probably only be worth running as economical daily transport until the MoT runs out and cannot be economically renewed — or, dare one suggest, as sources of hard-to-find body and trim spares to keep better specimens on the road.

It won't be worth much trouble or expense to restore an early 1600, for example, even if it is a rarer GT. The wide interchangeability of mechanical spares between all models, however, not to mention the inherent reliability of Ford mechanicals, means that very few running-gear problems will actually force a Capri off the road for good.

Start with a close look at the bodywork. Like most Fords of the period, it's a relatively simple structure which is generally easy enough to repair (remanufactured replacement panels are becoming increasingly available to supplant the ever-rarer obsolete Ford items), but it clearly pays to avoid serious corrosion. Despite their external differences, both MkI cars and later hatchbacks are very similar under the skin, and the same basic checks apply to both.

Front wings rust in all the usual places where mud has been allowed to accumulate and retain moisture against the metalwork. Check above and to the sides of the headlamps, the vertical joint between each wing and the lower front valance (itself worth a look for perforation, in addition to the inevitable stone chips), and the flat areas just to the sides of the bonnet.

Check the security of the stiffeners running between the top rear part of the wheelarch edges and the inner wings, and then have a good look at the top rear corner of each wing. Mud collects on an unseen ledge below this area and can eventually rot not only the wing but also the bulkhead behind it, after which it's only a matter of time before the door pillars — and even the floorpan below — go exactly the same way. The trailing edges of the

Above: The first thing any Capri buyer must look for is usually simple enough to spot — rust. The leading edge of the bonnet and the wing over the head-lamp are common trouble spots. Like virtually all the car's structural problems, they apply right across the range.

Above: Later cars aren't usually quite so bad, but it will still pay to have a close look at the metalwork below the headlamps, and the seams between the wings and the lower front valance. Neglected bumpers may well be rusty, too.

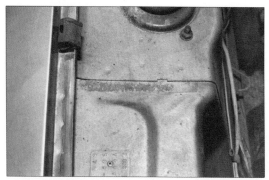

Above: Under the bonnet the most likely problem areas will be the inner wings round the top mountings for the MacPherson suspension struts. Even if all seems well, look carefully for signs of past repair and then have another look from beneath the wheelarches with a powerful torch.

wings are prone to corrosion, too, particularly at their lower corners where they take the full force of the continuous shot-blasting from the wheels.

Open the bonnet to examine the inner front wings. The joint with each outer wing, just below each side of the bonnet, is a vulnerable rust spot; so are the top mountings for the front suspension MacPherson struts. There should be no sign whatsoever of bubbling metal, holes or filler anywhere near the three strut mounting bolts, and ideally no sign of past repairs — though this is probably a little less than realistic on all but the most recent of cars.

Plating in this area is quite permissible provided it's been done properly: with a correctly shaped repair panel and continuous welding. Tack-welding, rivets and self-tapping screws are definitely not allowed, however. Prod the metal with a thin screwdriver to find the slightest weakness, and then have a look from beneath with a torch, first to make sure that any repair panel hasn't been simply patched over existing rust, and secondly that the vital strut-turret strengthening webs are still intact.

Inner and outer sills are a typical problem area, but usually only on badly neglected cars more than about ten years old. Check the entire length of each outer panel for the usual signs of repairs again (cover sills tacked over rust, holes, filler, fresh under-body sealant etc) and make sure that the drain holes at the base of each sill member where the outer skin meets the inner have not become blocked. Poke them clear with a piece of wire and, if you buy the car, keep them that way.

Test the strength of the jacking points next: ideally by jacking the car up on them, if the owner agrees (but at the same time never venturing beneath it unless it's also supported by stands), or at the very least by placing a stout iron bar in each one and discreetly attempting to prise it off the car. (With luck you won't succeed!) Then lift the carpets to check the inner sills, particularly where they meet the edges of the floorpan, and also round the all-important seat-belt mounting points.

Rear wheelarches often begin to bubble where water has found its way between the inner and outer panels, and in really bad cases the problem will extend to the lower rear corners of the wings, behind the wheels, and the rear ends of the sills where they meet the lower front corners of the wings. Repair is neither too difficult nor too expensive if the problem is caught in time: the offending corrosion is simply cut out of both inner and outer arches, and repair panels let in. Again, though, it's a problem best avoided if you can.

Have a look under the car, working your way along the longitudinal box-section strengtheners welded to the underside of the floor. At the very front, check where the vertical front panel meets the chassis sections near the attachment points for the anti-roll bar, then check the security of the crossmember to which the anti-roll bar itself is bolted.

The box-section members are also susceptible to rot just to the rear of each front wheel and where they kick up over the rear axle: make sure you look at both the outside and inside faces. In the same area, have a good dig at the metalwork in the vicinity of the four rear leaf-spring mounting points: rot here is both depressingly common and all too often concealed beneath an outwardly reassuring layer of under-body sealant. It's easy enough to repair, however.

Inside the car, lift out the rear-seat base and as much of the floor coverings as you can to ensure that the floorpan itself is still sound and that the metal directly above those 'U'-section strengthening channels beneath the floor hasn't rotted away.

Make sure you look right up under the fascia at its outer ends adjacent to the inner door pillars. Rotten pillars are common, and while the most obvious corrosion, normally easily visible when you open the door itself, may well have been concealed beneath layers of glassfibre and paint, rot in this under-dash area is much harder to hide. Check the door pillar area from under the front wings, too; and remember that, ideally, the wings themselves have to come off to make a good job of the repair. In really bad cases even the windscreen pillars will be seriously weakened, and a car as corroded as this should be avoided at all costs.

Doors rot upwards from their lower edges if the vital drain holes are blocked — check both the outer skin and the harder-to-see inner framework by getting down on your hands and knees if necessary — and remember that it's not unknown for

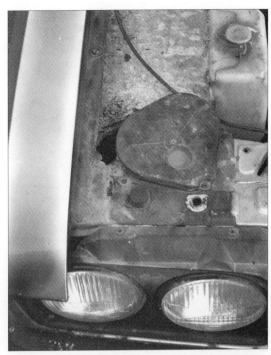

In some cases you'll find holes in the forward part of each inner wing round the access panels for the headlamp bulbs. This isn't in itself too serious, but does suggest that there are probably more horrors lurking beneath the shine.

the window frames to rot at their lower corners, often to the extent that the top part of the frame itself breaks right off the rest of the door.

Have a good look round the hinge area to make sure rust in the door pillars hasn't spread to the doors, too, and give each panel a firm shake up and down to test the hinges. Wear is by no means unusual (the Capri has very heavy doors which exert considerable leverage on the pins), but replacement is straightforward.

Bonnets occasionally rot along their leading edges, and boot lids and tailgates along their lower rear edges, but this isn't too serious a problem if you can find a reasonable secondhand replacement. Annoying and painful, too, is the tendency of the opening tailgate to crash back down onto your head once it's been opened, but this can be easily cured by a new set of support struts.

Worn, damaged or missing trim is clearly not the sort of difficulty which will keep a Capri off the road, but it can spoil your enjoyment of it, particularly if it is a rare and/or historically significant

Left: If the Capri's body shell has one major weakness, it lies in the door pillars. Even where the top of each pillar appears sound, it's not at all unlikely that you'll find rampant corrosion like this. It's difficult to repair this sort of damage properly, so your wisest option is simply to look for a better car.

Below, left and right: Don't be taken in by this perhaps harmless-looking patch of rust in the top rear corner of a front wing (left). Left to its own devices, the accumulated mud which caused it will eat away at the wing, the inner wing beneath it, and ultimately even the base of the windscreen pillar (right).

Above: The trailing edges of the front wings rust where mud and moisture have built up in the crevice between the inner and outer skins, and the doors suffer for much the same reason, particularly where the drain holes have been allowed to remain blocked for long periods. Wings are welded on rather than bolted, so repair isn't particularly easy.

Above: As the lowest part of the body, and subject to a continual barrage of mud, stones and water from the wheels, the sills are highly susceptible to corrosion. It's usually obvious when they become this bad (the photo shows the base of the 'B' post and the front of the rear quarter panel), but you should check the entire length of each sill for the slightest sign of weakened metal.

Right: Don't forget to lift the carpets to check the footwells and inner sills, the latter helpfully provided with holes through which you can assess their internal condition. The joint between the inner sill and the floorpan is particularly vulnerable, especially at the front end where it meets the base of the 'A' post area.

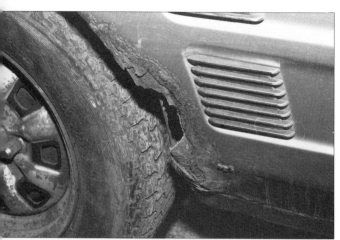

Above: Rear wheelarches rust badly where water has worked its way between the inner and outer panels, the damage often extending right down to the sills at the front and the lower valance at the rear. A proper repair involves fairly major surgery rather than the all-too-common layer of filler which has been tried on this Capri II (lower picture).

Above: Mk I boot lids rust where water collects in the lower rear seam. This one, removed from the car for clarity, is so badly affected that a secondhand replacement — assuming one can be found — is the only practicable answer.

model. Essentially the problems are straight-forward wear and tear, and sometimes the absence of specific items.

Carpets are easy to replace with material of a similar colour (texture can occasionally be a problem, although you should be able to find something fairly close), but do check the seats — not forgetting the backs of the front seats — for rips, wear patches and the inevitable cigarette burns. Check the seat adjustment mechanism, and check that the front-seat back hasn't collapsed altogether. In all cases, secondhand replacements are probably the cheapest answer, although a competent vehicle trimmer can often work wonders on the original damaged items.

The door trim panels are worth careful scrutiny. Dirt and wear are their principal enemies, but quite often you'll find that they have also warped badly, particularly along their lower edges where they tend to retain moisture. This can usually be overcome by carefully peeling back the vinyl covering material and pressing the dampened inner panel back into shape with a moderately hot iron. The intricate patterns on the vinyl cover will be virtually impossible to reproduce, however, so if they are damaged you'll have to be sure you can find secondhand replacements or else make do with plainer home-made covers.

And don't forget the headlining. You'll find that this is almost invariably torn and/or badly stained by cigarette smoke, particularly above the driver's seat, and the perforated vinyl material which Ford used throughout the 1970s is impossible to obtain. That won't stop you having a new headlining made up by a specialist trimmer, possibly in a better material, but it won't be original. Check the various door and window sealing rubbers, too. Long-term leaks wreak havoc on the interior trim and, more seriously, the hidden depths of the floorpan.

There's no great problem as far as glass is concerned, even for the early MkI cars, but don't under-estimate the cost of replacing cracked or broken panes. (Always replace a toughened windscreen with a laminated one if you can.) It's also worth making sure that the heated rear window (if fitted) works properly and that the door windows wind up and down smoothly. Rectifying what might appear to be minor problems like these can add considerably to the cost and time involved in getting a car back into service.

Brightwork, not surprisingly, has long been scarce for the MkI cars, and is not getting any easier for the later ones, either. MkI bumpers, door handles and badges are difficult, and the larger rear-lamp units so characteristic of the facelift MkI are simply unobtainable new and becoming ever-harder and more expensive to find secondhand. (They look initially like straightforward chrome-plated metal castings, but in fact they are made entirely of clear plastic with the chrome effect applied from the inside.) Check the headlamps for correct operation, and ensure that the silvering isn't peeling off the reflectors. The rectangular lamps used on early MkIs and the slightly larger units found on facelift cars are scarce and expensive, while the four 5 3/4-inch units of the MkIII are no problem at all.

Wheels can offer one or two minor but potentially irritating problems. There are plenty of aftermarket alternatives (of varying quality) to the standard Ford fare, but original-specification items in good condition can be hard to find. Four-spoked RS alloy wheels are very scarce and expensive, of course, so check them carefully for kerbing and corrosion damage, or signs of locking wheelnuts (always a good idea as long as you don't lose the key...) being chiselled off at some time in the past. The so-called pepperpot-style alloys of the 2.8 Injection look good on any model (with the right tyres) and are still available either new from Ford or secondhand from many wheel specialists.

Avoid cars which have been 'tuned' simply by the fitment of massively wide wheels and tyres, particularly if the required clearance has been obtained with spacers. The wheel bearings and many suspension components will have shorter working lives because of the extra stresses placed on them, and you'll almost certainly run into problems of tyres fouling on the wheelarches. Likewise it pays to be suspicious of cars festooned with all sorts of add-on GRP body-styling panels, particularly if they seem to be a recent addition to a car which is otherwise in below-average condition. They could simply be the start of an abandoned renovation project; then again, they could have been thrown together to hide all sorts of structural horrors.

Above: You can often expect to find quite major corrosion in the tailgate area of the later cars, too. If it's confined to the tailgate itself — usually where water has collected at the lower corners of the window — this is no great problem as replacements are still easy to find. Rust in the hinge area in the roof, however, is rather more serious.

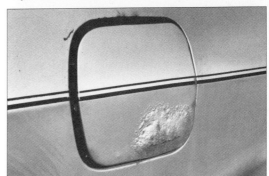

Above: Rust on petrol filler flaps is common and, while not in itself too serious, probably indicates that the car hasn't been particularly well cared for. Tread carefully.

Above: Brightwork for the earlier cars is hard to find, and rear lamp units for the post-1972 facelifted cars just about impossible. The lens assembly is, in fact, a single translucent colour moulding, the chrome effect round the edge created by a layer of silver paint applied from the inside.

Left: The single-overhead-camshaft Pinto engine is effectively the definitive Capri power unit and, with the right expertise and parts, can be made to propel the car very quickly indeed. Watch for oil leaks from the camshaft cover gasket, and change the camshaft drive belt as a preventive measure when you buy the car.

Below: Camshaft and associated valvegear wear was for many years a common problem on the Pinto engine. Regular oil and filter changes minimised the catastrophic wear of the camshaft lobes (left), but it was no use at all fitting new parts without at the same time renewing the spraybar (often blocked) which supplied vital lubricant to the camshaft. The cylinder head must be removed to do the job, but it's reasonably straightforward.

WHAT TO LOOK FOR • 23

Mechanically, Capris are about as sound and simple as you can get, and the ready availability of spares, both new and secondhand for all models, makes full-scale repairs easy.

Manual gearboxes sometimes have worn bearings and a weak second-gear synchromesh, but otherwise the change quality should be as good as you would expect of a rear-wheel-drive Ford (although the rod-change mechanism used on some models can occasionally be rather sloppy). Check for jumping out of gear on the over-run by deliberately snapping the throttle open and shut a few times. A similar technique in second gear will show up any clonks from the propshaft and differential, otherwise just listen for the tell-tale howl of a worn crown wheel and pinion — which, if you're lucky, may well be nothing more serious than worn rear wheel bearings. (Even if the diff has failed it should be easy enough to find a complete axle — for all but the LSD-equipped cars — in a breaker's yard.)

Relatively few four-cylinder Capris were equipped with Ford's own three-speed automatic gearbox, but that's no reason to avoid an automatic if it's at the right price and bodily sound. It's a good unit, and although it might take the edge off the acceleration it also makes the car very relaxing to drive, particularly in heavy traffic. Despite its apparent complexity it's also very reliable, and has the added benefit of somewhat cushioning the rest of the drivetrain and prolonging its life. It was always a more popular option on the bigger-engined models.

Check that the automatic gearbox changes up and down as it should without too much slip or harshness between each ratio, and make sure that you have reverse, of course. Repeat the test using the shift lever itself to control the speed of upward changes, and then have a look at the fluid. It should be a pink, clean-looking liquid, and if it contains black particles and smells like rotten eggs (indicating that the transmission has been overheated at some time) then you can reckon on needing a new or overhauled unit fairly soon.

Make all the usual checks for free play at the steering wheel — there shouldn't be any — and bounce all four corners of the car up and down to test the dampers. (Pulling to the left or right may be due to the top strut mounts being tightened with the wheels pointing to one side or the other.) Rear springs sometimes crack, and they often sag under sustained harsh acceleration — more of a problem on the bigger-engined models, of course — so make sure the car sits square on the road both front to back and side to side.

Brakes should be more than adequate unless the engine has been substantially tuned with no thought given to stopping (or unless the car has been persistently neglected), and again parts are easy enough to find for most of the range (except the RS3100). Common problems include a rather unresponsive, dead feel to the pedal (usually caused by the front caliper pistons sticking), and sometimes you'll encounter a rather worrying snaking when you brake hard. This was a common problem in the early days of the MkI 3.0-litre cars, and can usually be cured by making sure the hydraulic pipe runs to all four wheels are the same length.

A front suspension vibration on the 2.8 points to a warped disc, but don't discount causes like worn wheel bearings or softened track-control arm bushes. Anti-roll bar bushes wear quite quickly, too, and are a pain to fit without a special Ford tool, but it won't cost too much to have a garage do the work for you. A rather disquieting sensation that the rear of the car isn't quite connected to the front may also be due to worn bushes — in this case at each end of each spring and at the outer ends of the anti-roll bar, and also where the bar itself is secured to the rear-axle casing. MkI cars have two radius arms locating the axle instead of the anti-roll bar, but the principle (and effect) is the same.

Left: Major problem on the V4 and Essex V6 was blown head gaskets, sometimes accompanied by tiny but disastrous cracks in the castings. Check carefully for excess pressure in the cooling system, which must also contain anti-freeze to prevent corrosion and the build-up of sludge which leads to overheating.

Below: Standard Ford/Weber carburettors can wear after high mileages, leading to poor fuel consumption and erratic idling, but replacements are readily available. Automatic chokes often give trouble, too, so fit a manual system if you can.

Below: Bounce all four corners of the car up and down to check the suspension dampers — it should oscillate no more than twice — and then from beneath check the dampers for leaking fluid. The same applies to the inserts used in the front struts.

Which engine?

What goes wrong?

Such was the wide variety of engines used throughout the Capri's life that for the sake of clarity we've shown the relatively few specific weaknesses of the UK-market units in the easy-to-read lists on the next pages.

Needless to say, your first task should, in any case, be to check for all the usual problems found in ageing, neglected and/or abused power units: oil and coolant leaks (crankshaft and water-pump seals respectively), blue oil smoke in the exhaust, low oil pressure combined with main- and big-end bearing wear, excessive mechanical noise, misfiring, lack of power and so on.

If you're looking at more recent cars, ask to see a service history (always a good indication of how well it's been looked after) and, although the all-iron construction of all Capri engines makes them resistant to problems of internal cooling-system corrosion, make sure there is anti-freeze in the radiator. A compression test is a good idea, if the owner agrees, and could alert you to possible valve and/or cylinder head gasket problems.

All Ford engines will stand up to a great deal of wear and tear, and even deliberate abuse, and are among the easiest to rebuild when even they will run no more, but naturally it's best to avoid problems if you possibly can. Look for obvious signs of caring and careful regular maintenance, but at the same time don't turn down an otherwise immaculate car merely because the engine is a little noisy: repairing that will cost a fraction of even the most basic bodywork or interior trim restoration.

Above: Rear springs sag and/or crack, so check that the car sits level on the road. The bushes at each end also deteriorate with age, and replacing them may transform the car's road behaviour. Careful use of a screwdriver should show up any looseness.

Above: Anti-roll bar bushes don't last very long and can again have a serious effect on the car's normally good roadholding. The bushes fixing the bar itself to the body are no great problem (top), but you'll really need a special tool to fit the bushes at the outer ends of the bar where they meet the suspension upright.

Above: If the owner will let you remove the wheels for a closer look at the suspension, you can also take the opportunity to look at the brakes. Check the discs for scoring and the pads for excessive wear (top) and the rear brake assembly (below) for the correct operation of the self-adjusting mechanism (where fitted). Check the drums and shoes for wear too, of course.

Above: Rear axle 'U' bolts occasionally work loose and are worth checking if, when driving the rear end of the car feels not to be joined to the front. The top left-hand corner of this picture shows the mounting point for one of the two trailing arms which help to locate the axle (replaced by an anti-roll bar on later examples). The rubber bushes warrant a check with that screwdriver again.

Four-cylinder overhead-valve Kent engines: 1298cc, 1599cc

❖ Piston/bore wear indicated by high oil consumption and noticeable fuming from breather system, oil filler cap and exhaust.

❖ Timing chain rattles noisily when worn. Replace — together with new sprockets — for a complete cure.

❖ Strong five-bearing crankshaft rarely wears bearings. Low oil pressure often caused by worn pump or faulty sender/gauge unit.

❖ Noisy valvegear may simply be excessive clearances, but camshaft followers can wear badly. Replace in set of eight with cam itself.

❖ What looks like head-gasket problem — oil in water and *vice versa*, and excessive pressure in radiator — may be due to cracked cylinder block, particularly if it's been over-bored in the quest for more power. You can fit liners, but it's better to find a complete new unit to rebuild. Good 1600cc 711M blocks are scarce and pricey in scrapyards, though.

Four-cylinder single-overhead-camshaft Pinto engines: 1593cc, 1993cc, 2300cc

❖ Biggest single problem is wear of the camshaft and followers caused by blocked feed pipe/spraybar and/ or missed oil and filter changes (albeit nowhere near as common as it used to be). All parts — camshaft, followers etc — must be replaced as a set, which involves removing cylinder head.

❖ Toothed rubber timing belt rarely breaks, but preventive replacement when you buy the car certainly isn't a bad idea.

❖ Oil leaks from the rather complicated camshaft cover and its gasket are not unknown. Use a new gasket each time you remove the cover, and don't over-tighten fixings.

❖ Rough running (particularly at idle) and poor fuel consumption may be due to nothing more serious than wear in Ford's own variable-venturi carburettor on later models. After-market conversions are readily available (and worth fitting to any Ford-carburettored Capri for fuel-consumption and reliability benefits, if not performance).

❖ Probably the best all-round Capri engine. It's reliable and reasonably powerful in standard two-litre form, and readily tunable (with easily available parts) to produce astonishing power outputs.

Overhead-valve V4: 1288cc, 1488cc, 1688cc, 1996cc

❖ Not the best engine in the world, but certainly not as bad as its reputation would have you believe; nor is it as complex as its counter-rotating balance shaft (to smooth out inherent roughness) would suggest. Not worth actively looking for, however, unless you're an enthusiast for automotive lost causes.

❖ Fibre timing gear can break up after high mileages and if engine overheats; best replaced by steel (noisy and expensive but vital for total reliability) on a preventive basis.

❖ Oil leaks and noisy valvegear can be a problem; parts are hard to find. Balance-shaft bearings can wear out.

❖ Oil-pump drives can fail, resulting loss of pressure quickly wrecking bottom-end bearings. Should again be replaced on a preventive basis.

Overhead-valve Essex V6: 2994cc, 3091cc (RS3100)

❖ Can suffer from overheating if radiator becomes blocked with silt (itself caused by lack of anti-freeze in coolant). Check visually for blowing head gaskets, confirm with compression check if necessary (which could also reveal cracked cylinder heads).

❖ Like V4, fibre timing gear can break up with disastrous results, and oil-pump drive can shear. Doesn't have V4's balance shafts and bearings to wear out, though.

❖ Biggest problem is undoubtedly current scarcity of parts, particularly pistons, and even for standard 3.0-litre unit. RS3100 parts very hard to come by.

❖ Valvegear rocker arms pivot round crude ball and post as standard. These can pull out of the heads under duress, and must be modified for any serious tuning.

Overhead-valve Cologne V6: 1999cc, 2294cc, 2520cc, 2637cc (RS2600), 2792cc

❖ No real vices apart from inevitable weakness of fibre timing gear. Differentiated from Essex unit by rear-mounted distributor. (On the Essex it's at the front.)

❖ Bosch fuel-injection system reliable and long-lasting. Rough running more likely due to blocked fuel filters and/or a faulty high-pressure pump than damaged or worn metering unit. A scrupulously clean fuel supply is vital, however.

❖ Water pumps can wear quickly if drive belt has been over-tightened. Pump body itself can crack if mounting bolts are tightened unevenly, too.

Above: Noise and/or vibration which originates directly under the car is possibly caused by an out-of-balance propeller shaft or, on later cars, a worn centre bearing. Universal joints wear, too, but can again be checked by carefully attempting to lever them apart with a screwdriver.

Above: Check all the steel brake pipes and flexible rubber hoses for signs of rust and perishing. Early 3.0-litre cars had a tendency to snake from side to side under heavy braking, but this can usually be cured by ensuring that the pipe runs to all four wheels are as near the same length as possible. A dead feel to the brake pedal is more than likely caused by seized pistons in the front brake calipers; a vibration through the pedal under braking to warped discs.

*Above: The Mk I 1600GT was just about capable of 100mph, but the first truly high-performance
Capri was the 107mph V4-engined 2000GT. This was always comparatively rare, though, and it
was the V6-engined 3000GT, with its 113mph top speed, which really captured the public's attention.
The 3000E shown here, launched in March 1970, was intended as a luxurious 'Executive' version
of the GT, but with a top speed of 120mph it was also considerably quicker.*

*Above: The first homologation-special Capri was the German-built (and ostensibly German-market-only) RS2600
launched in September 1970. Powered by a fuel-injected Cologne V6 of 2637cc, it was capable of a genuine
126mph and, thanks to some fairly simple suspension modifications, had roadholding to match. This and the
photograph on page 40 amply illustrate the specialist nature of the RS2600: the car shown here has no bumpers
at all and a set of distinctive aluminium wheels, while the one on page 40 has gained a set of quarter-bumpers
and appears to be sporting a set of four-spoke aluminium wheels like those used on the British RS3100.
Note the absence of dummy air-intakes on the rear quarters of both vehicles, though, and the contrasting
colour scheme. Early cars were silver and blue, later ones white and blue. (Capri Club International)*

3.   Production history

Although this book is concerned only with genuinely high-performance Capris, this section covers the entire range — from 1300 upwards — in an effort to provide a clearer and more comprehensive picture of the car's development over the years. It is arranged in straightforward chronological order and, where possible, shows both the start and finish dates for the production of each important model.

Although they are inevitably rather scarce in the UK, German-market cars are given some prominence here, too. Not only are they an important part of the Capri story, but they also offer an interesting alternative source of the earlier high-performance Capris — if you don't mind driving from the left, of course.

November 1968: pre-launch Capri production began in Britain (Halewood, Liverpool) and Germany (Cologne).

February 1969: Capri simultaneously released for sale to the public in UK and Germany. UK range consisted of 1300, 1300GT, 1600 and 1600GT, all with crossflow Kent engines; in Germany the range consisted of 1300, 1500, 1700GT and 2000, all with V4 engines. X, L and R trim packs available in permutations to suit buyer.

March 1969: the first (and only) V4-engined Capri for the British market — the 2000GT — was introduced.

May 1969: the first V6-engined Capri — the 108bhp 2300GT — was introduced for the German market, while all cars received bigger (13.6-gallon/ 62-litre) fuel tanks.

September 1969: production of V6-engined 3000 GT began.

October 1969: 3000GT released for sale in the UK. More powerful (125bhp) version of German 2300GT launched at Frankfurt Motor Show.

March 1970: Capri 3000E introduced at Geneva Motor Show featuring GT mechanical components and XLR trim pack, plus opening rear-side windows and push-button radio. Pre-production mockup of German-market RS2600 also displayed, featuring 150bhp fuel-injected engine, modified suspension and some lightweight GRP panels.

April 1970: Capri introduced to US market at New York Motor Show with two pairs of circular headlamps, impact-absorbing front and rear bumpers and initially with 1600cc crossflow Kent engine. A total of 275,000 Capris had been built to date.

September 1970: V6-engined RS2600 — the first fuel-injected Ford to be built in any quantity — was introduced to the German market, together with the V6-engined 2600GT which had the same maximum power as now-deleted 125bhp 2300GT, but more torque. (The 108bhp 2300GT remained in production.) In the UK, improvements for 1971 model year included more powerful 1300 and 1600

Left: The so-called facelift Capris were introduced in September 1972, essentially to keep an ageing design alive until the hatchback Capri II could be launched in 1974. Major distinguishing features were the larger rear lamps and rather ostentatious power bulge on the bonnet. Less noticeable, but no less important, were the fitting of the 1600 Pinto engine in place of the 1600 crossflow and, for the 3000, the use of a stronger German gearbox.

Below: At the same time as production of the Mk I Capri ceased, in September 1973, Ford built a small number of the RS3100. Although it featured an over-bored version of the Essex V6 engine, it was otherwise mechanically similar to the RS2600 and almost as fast. Note the large boot-mounted spoiler and, in contrast to the RS2600, the use of the standard Capri's dummy air-intake mouldings just in front of the rear wheels. (Capri Club International)

Below: The hatchback Capri II was introduced in February 1974 with mechanical components broadly similar to the earlier range but with an all-new body shell. This is a German-specification 2.3 Ghia (the twin exhaust tailpipes were a crude but effective way of identifying V6-engined cars), complete with the cast alloy road wheels used on many of the high-performance and luxury Capris until the 1980s. (Capri Club International)

First seen at the Geneva Motor Show in March 1975, the Capri S went on sale in Britain the following June. With 1.6-, 2.0- and 3.0-litre engines, all to GT specification, it initially featured special black paintwork with panels outlined in gold, black bumpers, door and window frames and door handles, and gold badging throughout. Inside there was a similar black treatment for all normally bright metal parts, and the almost inevitable black upholstery with gold-coloured cloth panels in the seats. A 2.3-litre version was available only in Germany; subsequently the all-black colour scheme was dropped. (Capri Club International)

Kent engines thanks to modified cylinder heads, valve timing and carburettor jets, plus servo-assisted brakes across the range and improved lights.

September 1971: V4-engined Capri Special introduced to UK market with 2000GT engine, Vista Orange paintwork and many extra items of trim as standard. Some 1200 were built.

October 1971: German RS2600 fitted with ventilated front disc brakes and stronger gearbox, plus slightly softer suspension and increased ride height, cast-alloy road wheels and quarter-bumpers. In UK, coachbuilders Crayford exhibited drophead Caprice at Earls Court Motor Show, and improvements to V6 engine (cylinder heads, exhaust manifolds, camshaft and carburettor jets) raised power to 138bhp to make 3000GT fastest production-built UK Ford at 122mph. Car also featured softer rear suspension, revised gear ratios,

higher final drive, improved cooling for front disc brakes and larger servo. Automatic fitted with viscous-coupled radiator cooling fan.

February 1972: GT models (1300, 1600 and 3000) dropped from UK range, apart from V4-engined 2000GT.

June 1972: limited run of 1600GT, 2000GT and 3000GT produced, all with high trim specification and special paintwork, plus bonnet bulge previously used only on 3.0-litre cars.

July 1972: 3000E dropped from UK range.

September 1972: so-called facelift Capris introduced with claimed 151 changes — major and minor — to specification. These included one-piece rear anti-roll bar instead of earlier twin radius arms, and softer but more progressive suspension

Rather less well-known were the tiny handful of early 'S'-specification cars with white paintwork and bumpers.(Capri Club International)

designed to give more wheel control over rough surfaces. All cars were fitted with the power-bulge bonnet and more powerful rectangular headlamps (except new 3000GXL which had four 5 3/4-inch round lamps), front indicator lamps mounted in the bumper and larger rear lamps. Inside there was a completely revised fascia, together with better seats which provided a useful increase in legroom for rear-seat passengers. The 1600 crossflow engine was dropped and replaced by Pinto unit of same nominal capacity. All 3000s had viscous-coupled fan and stronger German gearbox; automatic was optional on all but 1300s. Range rationalised to offer L, XL and GT models with GXL trim on 3000.

October 1972: German Capri range brought into line with earlier changes for UK market. V4 engine dropped and replaced by Pinto for 1300L and 1600XL or GT. German-designed V6 retained for 108bhp 2300GT and 2600GT, but UK-designed Essex V6 used in 3000GXL. Minor body and mechanical revisions for RS2600.

August 1973: the millionth Capri — an RS2600 — was built at Cologne.

December 1973: production of first-generation Capris ceased, and production of limited-edition RS3100 homologation special began at Halewood. Based on RS2600 mechanics (also discontinued at this time) and 3000GT body (with front airdam and quarter bumpers, four GXL-style headlamps and large rear spoiler), it had a 3.1-litre Essex engine developing 148bhp and was capable of 125mph.

January 1974: RS3100 production discontinued after about 1000 (many with incomplete specifications) assembled.

February 1974: second-generation Capris introduced with slightly longer, wider and heavier hatchback body shell and folding rear seat backs. Mechanical changes included larger front disc brakes, softer suspension, and alternator instead of earlier dynamo. UK range consisted of crossflow-engined 1300L, Pinto-engined 1600L, XL and GT, Pinto-engined 2000GT and new Ghia model, plus V6 3000GT and Ghia. Ford C3 automatic gearbox available as optional extra on some models, as was power steering. German range consisted of 1300L and XL, 1600L, XL and GT, 2300GT and Ghia, and 3000GT and Ghia. Crossflow-engined 1300GT exported to France and Italy only.

March 1975: Capri S in Midnight black paintwork with contrasting gold coachlining exhibited at Geneva Motor Show for sale in mainland Europe with 1.6-, 2.0-, 2.3- and 3.0-litre engines, gas-filled suspension dampers and cast-alloy road wheels.

June 1975: Capri S went on sale in UK with all but 2.3-litre engine.

October 1975: low-specification 1300 introduced for UK market with fixed rear seat backs and plain black trim while 1300L and 1600L received improved trim. XL models replaced by new GL specification, GT by new S, all assembled in Germany. Remote-control door mirror fitted to Ghia, power steering to 3.0-litre Ghia and S.

February 1976: Kent engines modified, and so-called Sonic Idle carburettor fitted to 1300 and 1600 to reduce fuel consumption. Automatic

Above: The third-generation Capris were introduced at the Geneva Show in March 1978, allegedly with something like 150 revisions to the mechanical and structural components, but in practice little different from their predecessors. The most obvious feature was the extended bonnet which seemed to give the head-lamps a sort of 'eyebrow' effect.
(Capri Club International)

Below: Three years later, in March 1981 and again in Geneva, the left-hand-drive-only 2.8 Injection appeared. It became available in Britain the following July at just under £8,000 and, with its near-130mph top speed, was an instant success. During the mid-1980s it became the definitive sporting Capri and, sadly, a favourite target for car thieves.
(Capri Club International)

At about the same time that the UK market belatedly received the 2.8 Injection, the German
market took another leap forward with the launch of the Zakspeed-engineered Capri Turbo (above).
It was a strange mixture of 2.8-litre carburettor-fed Granada engine with a KKK turbocharger,
2.8 Injection running gear and X-Pack body panels, and was clearly designed to bask in the
reflected glory of the highly successful Zakspeed racers (below). Only about 200 were built
and officially it was only ever available in Germany. (Photo above, Capri Club International)

transmission and tinted glass available on all but 1300.

March 1976: low-compression 1300 and 1600 introduced to German market with 54bhp and 68bhp respectively, plus new two-litre 90bhp V6.

October 1976: British Capri production discontinued at Halewood after 337,491 cars built there. All production transferred to Germany.

November 1976: minor modifications to S models included front airdam and rear spoiler to improve high-speed stability.

August 1977: production of Federal-specification Capri for US market discontinued at Cologne after total of 513,449 built.

March 1978: third-generation Capris (so-called Capri III) introduced at Geneva Show. All mechanically similar to equivalent Capri IIs, but body revisions included new grille, bumpers and front valance incorporating airdam, together with four headlamps and extended bonnet leading edge. Rear spoiler standard on S models, gas-filled rear dampers on all but 1300. UK range consisted of 1300L/ GL, 1600L/GL, 1600S, 2.0GL, S or Ghia and 3.0S or Ghia. German range was identical up to 1600, then included Pinto or V6 engine for 2.0 models, V6 for 2300S/Ghia and Essex V6 for 3.0S/Ghia.

April 1979: all cars fitted with viscous-coupled cooling fans and brake-fluid warning light; automatic choke fitted to 1.6-litre models, lower-profile tyres to 2.0-litres. Rear fog lamps fitted to L models, head restraints, passenger door mirror, remote-control driver's door mirror and headlamp washers to GL. S models fitted with rear fog lamps, driver's door mirror and improved under-bonnet sound insulation. Radio/cassette player fitted to Ghia as standard. In Germany, 2300 V6 uprated from 108 to 114bhp.

March 1980: GT4 limited-edition Capri introduced, based on 1600L but fitted with special seats, silver-painted sports road wheels and more comprehensive instrumentation.

October 1980: GL cars fitted with 5.5-inch road wheels (optional on L). Six-inch steel wheels with 185-section tyres standard on S models and optional on GL and Ghia.

January 1981: Recaro seats and revised interior trim fitted to S models; 1.6S replaced by 1.6LS featuring single-choke carburettor, sports wheels, spoiler on tailgate and centre console with clock. Ghia models now equipped with metallic paintwork, rear seat belts and stereo radio/cassette player. All cars now fitted with detachable rear parcel shelves.

March 1981: left-hand-drive Capri 2.8 Injection introduced at Geneva Motor Show for sale in mainland Europe.

July 1981: Capri 2.8 Injection launched in right-hand-drive form with four-speed manual gearbox for UK market. Turbocharged Zakspeed 2.8-litre Capri launched in Germany with wider wheelarches and large airdam and rear spoiler. Special-edition Cameo and Calypso Capris introduced, budget-priced Cameo based on 1.3 or 1.6L, high-specification Calypso on 1.6LS.

October 1981: Econolight fuel-saving system introduced on four-cylinder Capris.

May 1982: limited-edition Cabaret 1.6 introduced with sunroof, rear spoiler, GL-type road wheels, LS-style fabric seats, full instrumentation and optional two-litre engine.

October 1982: Tickford Capri exhibited at NEC Motor Show, featuring extensively modified bodywork and trim plus turbocharged 2.8-litre engine, limited-slip differential, rear disc brakes and 'A'-frame location for rear axle.

January 1983: five-speed gearbox introduced as standard equipment for 2.8 Injection and subsequently available on two-litre models. Cabaret II introduced, based on 1.6 or 2.0L models but with Recaro seats as used in the 2.8 Injection models, tinted glass, opening rear side windows and 185/70 tyres as standard.

Above: At the other end of the performance scale, May 1982 saw the launch of the limited-edition Cabaret. Based on a 1.6LS-specification car, it featured a tailgate spoiler, GL sports road wheels and full instrumentation and, as an extra-cost option, could also be had with a 2.0-litre Pinto engine. The Cabaret II, introduced in January 1983, came with Recaro seats like those in the 2.8 Injection, tinted glass, and wider wheels and tyres.

Below: Heart of the exotic Tickford Turbo, launched at the NEC Motor Show in October 1982 and on sale from September 1983, was a turbocharged version of the basic 2.8 Injection engine developing just over 200bhp. Bodywork and trim were extensively modified, too, while underneath the car featured a limited-slip differential, 'A'-frame location for the rear axle, and disc brakes on all four wheels. The Tickford was capable of 140mph.

March 1983: Capri range rationalised to consist of 1.6LS, 2.0S and 2.8 Injection; L, GL and Ghia discontinued. LS featured sunroof, improved suspension, better seats, and four-speed gearbox. S had five-speed Sierra-type gearbox, sunroof and new interior trim with XR3-style seats, improved suspension and opening rear side windows.

September 1983: Tickford Capri put on sale.

June 1984: special-edition Laser models introduced with 1.6- or 2.0-litre engines and various trim revisions.

October 1984: Capri range further rationalised to leave just Laser models and new 2.8 Injection Special, the latter featuring leather interior trim panels, rear seat belts, limited-slip differential and RS spoked alloy wheels. Tickford Capri production continued at some three cars per week with slight modifications to ignition and cooling systems.

November 1984: production of all left-hand-drive Capris ceased.

January 1986: further improvements made to Tickford Capri, including central locking plus new paint, badging and fascia.

June 1986: Turbo Technics Capri introduced at selected Ford dealers. Based on 2.8 Injection but had turbocharged engine producing some 200bhp and improved suspension and brakes.

December 1986: last Capris built at Cologne, including 1038 special-edition Capri 280 models with Brooklands Green metallic paint, leather seats and 50-series tyres on cast-alloy road wheels. Final Capri total was 1,886,647.

March 1987: final batch of Capri 280 models introduced in UK, with the last one sold towards the end of the year.

Above: In October 1984 the Capri range was rationalised to leave just the limited-edition Laser and the Injection Special. The main features of the latter were a limited-slip differential, spoked RS wheels, leather trim and rear seat belts. The following month production of left-hand-drive Capris ceased, and from then on the car was available only in Britain.

Below: By 1986 the Capri's days were numbered. In June turbocharger specialists Turbo Technics began to offer their blown 2.8 Injection through selected Ford dealers (the Tickford was still in production, but only just), and the following December production of all Capris came to an end after just over 18 years. (Capri Club International)

Above: Mk I 1600GT

Below: Mk I 2000GT (V4)

Below: Mk I 3000GT

4. Facts & figures

The eight Capris for which we've listed the most pertinent technical information for prospective buyers were themselves selected as being the most relevant to that same would-be owner. They are all capable of at least 100mph (albeit only just in the case of the MkI 1600GT) and, between them, they represent the easiest and most cost-effective way of acquiring one of these fine cars with the sort of performance to match its looks.

Apart from the highly prized RS2600 built in Germany (if anything, even more desirable than the otherwise similar British-built RS3100), we have deliberately not covered any of the German-market-only high-performers. German-market cars have always been rare on this side of the English Channel anyway, and even the high-profile turbo-charged 2.8-litre Zakspeed cars, while a little more numerous than our own Tickford, were essentially low-volume specials and not really representative of the marque as a whole.

As the years passed, even the most basic 1.6- or 2.0-litre cars came to be capable of the magic ton, hence the inclusion of the MkII/III 2.0S, but they had none of the essential character which makes the 99mph MkI 1600GT so enjoyable to drive even now.

We're sorry, then, if your own favourite isn't included; and sorry, too, if your own facts and figures tell a different story. It's never easy compiling this sort of information up to 20 years after the event, and in many cases no two sources give exactly the same information for reliable cross-checking. What follows is, however, as accurate as you'll find anywhere.

MkI 1600GT

Engine type: 'Kent' longitudinally mounted in-line four, with water cooling and two pushrod-operated overhead valves per cylinder. Cast-iron cylinder head and block with five-bearing crankshaft.
Bore: 80.9mm
Stroke: 77.6mm
Capacity: 1599cc
Compression ratio: 9.2:1
Fuel system: twin-choke Weber 32DFM carburettor (early models) or twin-choke Weber 32/36DGV/DGAV carburettor (later models).
Power: 86bhp at 5500rpm
Torque: 92lb/ft at 4000rpm
Transmission: dry, single-plate cable-operated clutch with four-speed manual gearbox. Final-drive ratio 3.77:1.
Suspension: MacPherson struts incorporating telescopic shock absorbers, lower track-control arms and anti-roll bar at front; semi-elliptic leaf springs with two radius arms and telescopic shock absorbers at rear.
Steering: rack-and-pinion
Brakes: hydraulically operated 9.625-inch diameter front discs and 9 x 1.75-inch rear drums.
Wheels and tyres: 165 x 13-inch radial tyres on 5-inch sculptured steel sports wheels.
Length: 169.5 inches   **Width:** 64.5 inches
Height: 50.7 inches   **Wheelbase:** 100.8 inches
Unladen weight: 2024lbs/920kg

Typical Performance
Maximum speed: 99mph   **0-60mph:** 13.4 secs
Standing quarter mile: 18.8 secs
Average fuel consumption: 25mpg

Above: RS2600 (Capri Club International)   *Below: RS3100 (Capri Club International)*

MkI 2000GT V4

Engine type: longitudinally mounted 60-degree V4, with water cooling and two pushrod-operated overhead valves per cylinder. Cast-iron cylinder heads and block with three-bearing crankshaft and single counter-rotating balance shaft.
Bore: 93.7mm
Stroke: 72.4mm
Capacity: 1996cc
Compression ratio: 8.9:1
Fuel system: twin-choke Weber 32/36DFV carburettor (manual choke) or twin-choke Weber 32/36DFAV carburettor (automatic choke).
Power: 93bhp at 5500rpm
Torque: 103lb ft at 3600rpm
Transmission: dry, single-plate cable-operated clutch and four-speed manual gearbox. Final-drive ratio 3.54:1 to October 1970, 3.44:1 thereafter.
Suspension: MacPherson struts incorporating telescopic shock absorbers, lower track-control arms and anti-roll bar at front; semi-elliptic leaf springs with two radius arms and telescopic shock absorbers at rear. (Rear radius arms replaced by anti-roll bar after September 1972.)
Steering: rack-and-pinion
Brakes: hydraulically operated 9.625-inch diameter front discs and 9 x 1.75-inch rear drums.
Wheels and tyres: 165 x 13-inch radial tyres on 5-inch sculptured steel sports wheels.
Length: 169.5 inches
Width: 64.5 inches
Height: 50.7 inches
Wheelbase: 100.8 inches
Unladen weight: 2112lbs/960kg

Typical Performance
Maximum speed: 107mph   **0-60mph:** 10.6 secs
Standing quarter mile: 18.2 secs
Average fuel consumption: 23mpg

MkI 3000GT

Engine type: 'Essex' longitudinally mounted 60-degree V6, with water cooling and two pushrod-operated overhead valves per cylinder. Cast-iron cylinder heads and block with four-bearing crankshaft. No balance shaft.
Bore: 93.7mm
Stroke: 72.4mm
Capacity: 2994cc
Compression ratio: 8.9:1
Fuel system: twin-choke Weber 40DFAV carburettor until October 1971; twin-choke Weber 38DGAS carburettor thereafter.
Power: 136bhp at 4750rpm
Torque: 181lb/ft at 3000rpm
Transmission: dry, single-plate cable-operated clutch and four-speed manual gearbox. Final-drive ratio 3.22:1 (3.09:1 after October 1971).
Suspension: MacPherson struts incorporating telescopic shock absorbers, lower track-control arms and anti-roll bar at front; semi-elliptic leaf springs with two radius arms and telescopic shock absorbers at rear. (Rear radius arms replaced by anti-roll bar after September 1972).
Steering: rack-and-pinion
Brakes: hydraulically operated 9.625-inch diameter front discs and 9 x 1.75-inch rear drums.
Wheels and tyres: 185 x 13-inch steel-belted radial tyres on 5-inch sculptured steel sports wheels.
Length: 168.5 inches
Width: 64.8 inches
Height: 50.7 inches
Wheelbase: 100.8 inches
Unladen weight: 2370lbs/1075kg

Typical Performance
Maximum speed: 113mph   **0-60mph:** 10.3 secs
Standing quarter mile: 17.6 secs
Average fuel consumption: 21mpg

RS2600

Engine type: 'Cologne' longitudinally mounted 60-degree V6, with water cooling and two pushrod-operated overhead valves per cylinder. Cast-iron cylinder heads and block with four-bearing crankshaft.
Bore: 90mm
Stroke: 69mm
Capacity: 2637cc
Compression ratio: 10.5:1
Fuel system: Kugelfischer mechanical fuel-injection system modified by Weslake and Ford AVO (Advanced Vehicle Operations). Some cars fitted with carburettors.

Power: 150bhp at 5800rpm
Torque: 165lb/ft at 3500rpm
Transmission: dry, single-plate hydraulically operated clutch with four-speed manual gearbox. Final-drive ratio 3.22:1 (3.09:1 after October 1971).
Suspension: essentially as for 3000GT but with negative-camber front crossmember, stiffer gas-filled shock absorbers, shorter coil springs and thicker anti-roll bar at front; single-leaf semi-elliptic springs at rear with gas-filled shock absorbers, progressive bump stops and anti-roll bar. (Prototypes had radius arms, but this was modified to anti-roll bar for volume production).
Steering: rack-and-pinion
Brakes: hydraulically operated 9.625-inch front discs (ventilated 9.75-inch discs after September 1973) and 9 x 2.25-inch rear drums.
Wheels and tyres: 6J x 13-inch cast-alloy road wheels by Minilite, Richard Grant or Ford AVO with 185/70 HR radial tyres.
Length: 169.5 inches
Width: 64.5 inches
Height: 49.7 inches
Wheelbase: 100.8 inches
Unladen weight: 1980lbs (900kg) to 2376lbs (1080kg)

Typical Performance
Maximum speed: 126mph
0-60mph: 7.3 secs
Standing quarter mile: 15 secs
Average fuel consumption: 20mpg

RS3100

Engine type: 'Essex' longitudinally mounted 60-degree V6, with water cooling and two pushrod-operated overhead valves per cylinder. Cast-iron cylinder heads and block with four-bearing crankshaft. No balance shaft.
Bore: 95.19mm
Stroke: 72.4mm
Capacity: 3091cc
Compression ratio: 9:1
Fuel system: twin-choke Weber 38EGAS carburettor
Power: 148bhp at 5000rpm
Torque: 187lb/ft at 3000rpm
Transmission: dry, single-plate cable-operated clutch and four-speed manual gearbox. Final-drive ratio 3.09:1.
Suspension: essentially as for 3000GT but with

negative-camber front crossmember, stiffer gas-filled shock absorbers, shorter coil springs and thicker anti-roll bar at front; single-leaf semi-elliptic springs at rear with gas-filled shock absorbers, progressive bump stops and anti-roll bar.
Steering: rack-and-pinion
Brakes: hydraulically operated 9.75-inch ventilated front discs and 9 x 2.25-inch rear drums.
Wheels and tyres: 6J x 13-inch Ford AVO four-spoke cast-alloy road wheels and 185/70HR radial tyres.
Length: 169.5 inches
Width: 64.5 inches
Height: 49.72 inches
Wheelbase: 100.8 inches
Unladen weight: 2310lbs/1050kg

Typical Performance
Maximum speed: 125mph
0-60mph: 7.2 secs
Standing quarter mile: 15.7 secs
Average fuel consumption: 22mpg

MkII/III 2.0S

Engine type: 'Pinto' longitudinally mounted in-line four, with water cooling and two overhead valves per cylinder operated by belt-driven overhead camshaft. Cast-iron cylinder head and block with five-bearing crankshaft.
Bore: 90.8mm
Stroke: 76.9mm
Capacity: 1993cc
Compression ratio: 9.2:1
Fuel system: twin-choke Weber carburettor
Power: 98bhp at 5500rpm
Torque: 111lb/ft at 3500rpm
Transmission: dry, single-plate cable-operated clutch with four-speed manual gearbox. Final-drive ratio 3.44:1.
Suspension: MacPherson struts, coil springs and anti-roll bar at front; semi-elliptic multiple-leaf springs and anti-roll bar at rear, with gas-filled shock absorbers from 1976.
Steering: rack-and-pinion
Brakes: hydraulically operated 9.625-inch front discs and 9 x 2.25-inch rear drums.
Wheels and tyres: 5J x 13-inch cast-alloy wheels with 185/70 radial-ply tyres.
Length: 171 inches

Width: 67 inches
Height: 51 inches
Wheelbase: 101 inches
Unladen weight: 2335lbs/1061kg

Typical Performance
Maximum speed: 107mph
0-60mph: 10.8 secs
Standing quarter mile: 17.7 secs
Average fuel consumption: 25mpg

MkII/III 3.0S

Engine type: 'Essex' longitudinally mounted 60-degree V6, with water cooling and two pushrod-operated overhead valves per cylinder. Cast-iron cylinder head and block with four-bearing crankshaft. No balance shaft.
Bore: 93.7mm
Stroke: 72.4mm
Capacity: 2994cc
Compression ratio: 9:1
Fuel system: Weber twin-choke carburettor
Power: 138bhp at 4750rpm
Torque: 174lb/ft at 3000rpm
Transmission: dry, single-plate cable-operated clutch and four-speed manual gearbox. Final-drive ratio 3.09:1.
Suspension: MacPherson struts, coil springs and anti-roll bar at front; semi-elliptic multiple-leaf springs and anti-roll bar at rear, with gas-filled shock absorbers from 1976.
Steering: power-assisted rack-and-pinion
Brakes: hydraulically operated 9.75-inch front discs and 9 x 2.25-inch rear drums.
Wheels and tyres: 5.5J x 13-inch cast-alloy wheels with 185/70 radial-ply tyres.
Length: 169 inches
Width: 67 inches
Height: 51 inches
Wheelbase: 101 inches
Unladen weight: 2574lbs/1168kg

Typical Performance
Maximum speed: 117mph
0-60mph: 9.0 secs
Standing quarter mile: 17.0 secs
Average fuel consumption: 23mpg

2.8 injection

Engine type: 'Cologne' longitudinally mounted 60-degree V6, with water cooling and two pushrod-operated overhead valves per cylinder. Cast-iron cylinder heads and block with four-bearing crankshaft.
Bore: 93mm
Stroke: 68.5mm
Capacity: 2792cc
Compression ratio: 9.2:1
Fuel system: Bosch K-Jetronic fuel injection
Power: 150bhp at 5700rpm
Torque: 162lb/ft at 4300rpm
Transmission: dry, single-plate cable-operated clutch and four-speed manual gearbox; later cars fitted with five-speed manual gearbox. Final-drive ratio 3.09:1.
Suspension: MacPherson struts incorporating Bilstein gas-filled telescopic shock absorbers, lower track-control arms and anti-roll bar at front; single-leaf semi-elliptic springs with Bilstein gas-filled telescopic shock absorbers and anti-roll bar at rear.
Steering: power-assisted rack and pinion
Brakes: hydraulically operated ventilated 10.3-inch diameter front discs and 9 x 2.25-inch rear drums.
Wheels and tyres: cast-alloy 7J x 13-inch wheels with 205/60VR radial-ply tyres; later cars fitted with 7J x 15-inch wheels with 195/50VR radial tyres.
Length: 172 inches
Width: 67 inches
Height: 51 inches
Wheelbase: 101 inches
Unladen weight: 2620 lbs (1190kg)

Typical Performance
(four-speed cars;
five-speed cars in brackets)
Maximum speed: 127mph (125mph)
0-60mph: 7.9 secs (8.3 secs)
Standing quarter mile: 16.2 secs (16.3 secs)
Average fuel consumption: 21mpg (23mpg)

Mk II 2.0S
(Capri Club International)

Mark II 3.0S

2.8 Injection

What Have You Found?

It's always useful to be able to identify a prospective purchase from its chassis number or, after 1981, its EEC-style vehicle identification number (VIN). It might seem an arcane and potentially pointless exercise, but not only should it positively link the car to the details on the registration document (provided, of course, that some unscrupulous owner hasn't doctored either the car or the document; always bear this possibility in mind), but it can also provide a fairly clear picture of the mechanical specification and (sometimes) the optional equipment with which it left the factory.

That's invaluable if you are restoring an older and/or historically significant example which has clearly been substantially modified from its original but unknown specification, and the true date any car was built can be useful as far as ordering parts is concerned. (In some cases these may have been modified or updated during the model year rather than at the beginning.) Other details, such as the final-drive ratio, are useful if you are contemplating a tyre or rear-axle swop, while the paint and trim codes — though not fully explained here, because of lack of space — are essential if your aim is 100 per cent originality.

You'll find the chassis plate either on the transverse panel under the leading edge of the bonnet, or on the right-hand front inner wing. (US-market cars have an additional metal plate attached to the fascia on the driver's side just below the windscreen and visible from outside the vehicle.) It should be secured by rivets; be suspicious, unless perhaps the car has obviously been resprayed, if it's screwed on, or even if it simply doesn't look the right one for the car. Be warned, too, that the identifying letters and numbers are not always easy to read, particularly if the aluminium plate has begun to corrode. You'll sometimes have to make an educated guess, often based on what you know the figures are unlikely to be.

Neither are the characters always that easy to decode, so we make no apologies for not including an exhaustive guide to literally every type of chassis plate — and its contents — which you might conceivably find on a Capri. There are, if not actual errors in most other published 'ciphers', then inconsistencies at the very least, but the author, having personally used what follows to crack a number of randomly selected plates and match them to their cars, is reasonably satisfied that this one is as complete and accurate as can be expected.

Capris built before September 1972 had identification plates in English or German and, as such, clearly stated the car's country of origin. After that date, the plate was in English and German and the country of origin (Britain or Germany) could only be deduced from the identification number itself. Don't be too concerned by apparent blanks on the chassis plate. Front and rear axle loads, for example, initially tended to be given only for the German market, and braking system details only for Italy. There were also various apparently illogical variations under the Typ/Type heading for the French market, but they needn't concern us here.

On the other hand, there is also the added complication that in some cases characters in the Typ/Type box are apparently omitted without so much as a dash or 'X' to say so. The three plates we chose to illustrate Capri Mark 1 and ll numbers, for example, have ECJL, ECJUY and GECP respectively under the Type heading. This indicates, not surprisingly, that all three cars are Capris ('E') with two-door coupe bodies ('C'), but only the third gives any clue to the car's origin, in this case 'G' for Germany.

The two letter 'J's and the letter 'P' indicate the year each model was actually launched (J for 1969, P for 1974; note that as far as Ford itself is concerned there is no difference between the MkII, introduced in 1974, and the MkIII), and the L and UY of the first two numbers tells us the engine type which information is duplicated in the 'Motor/ Engine' panel. Simple, isn't it? (For the record, L indicates a 1.6-litre engine, type not shown here, and UY, on this French-registered car, a 2.6-litre overhead-valve V6. There's a full engine decoding chart below.)

Finally, to prove that you can take the search for your car's true identity a little too far, bear this in mind. While all chassis plates provide the not totally irrelevant information about the original position of the steering wheel (left- or right-hand drive, in other words), even the various European Ford divisions couldn't seem to agree on a

Left: Mk I chassis identification plates will look something like this, mounted on the right-hand front inner wing.

Below, left and right: This is the equivalent plate on a Mk II car, here mounted on the bonnet lock panel just inboard of the right-hand headlamp. Note the corrosion which is beginning to obscure some of the characters; also the rivets securing the plate to the body. Don't confuse the chassis plate proper with the body number plate (below right) which was for Ford's own use within the factory.

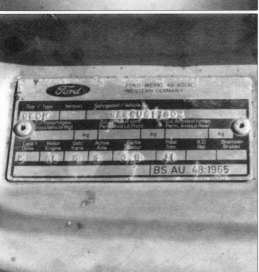

Left: Post-1981 cars had an EEC-style plate carrying what had by then become known as the Vehicle Identification Number, or VIN. Again it will be found on the bonnet lock panel.

Year of Production	Month of Production											
	JAN	FEB	MAR	APR	MAY	JUN	JUL	AUG	SEP	OCT	NOV	DEC
H — 1968											S	T
J — 1969	J	U	M	P	B	R	A	G	C	K	D	E
K — 1970	L	Y	S	T	J	U	M	P	B	R	A	G
L — 1971	C	K	D	E	L	Y	S	T	J	U	M	P
M — 1972	B	R	A	G	C	K	D	E	L	Y	S	T
N — 1973	J	U	M	P	B	R	A	G	C	K	D	E
P — 1974	L	Y	S	T	J	U	M	P	B	R	A	G
R — 1975	C	K	D	E	L	Y	S	T	J	U	M	P
S — 1976	B	R	A	G	C	K	D	E	L	Y	S	T
T — 1977	J	U	M	P	B	R	A	G	C	K	D	E
U — 1978	L	Y	S	T	J	U	M	P	B	R	A	G
W — 1979	C	K	D	E	L	Y	S	T	J	U	M	P
A — 1980	B	R	A	G	C	K	D	E	L	Y	S	T
B — 1981	J	U	M	P	B	R	A	G	C	K	D	E
C — 1982	L	Y	S	T	J	U	M	P	B	R	A	G
D — 1983	C	K	D	E	L	Y	S	T	J	U	M	P
E — 1984	B	R	A	G	C	K	D	E	L	Y	S	T
F — 1985	J	U	M	P	B	R	A	G	C	K	D	E
G — 1986	L	Y	S	T	J	U	M	P	B	R	A	G

consistent nomenclature. British-built Capris up to August 1970 had 1 or 2 under the 'Drive' heading to indicate right-or left-hand drive respectively but, just to confuse the issue, British Capris after that date and all German Capris use the opposite system. Here 1 (or A) stands for left-hand drive and 2 (or B) for right-hand drive. You have been warned!

The actual vehicle numbers we chose to illustrate the principles are as follows:

BBECNK34795
GCECNG56492
GAECUG17802

The first pair of letters indicates the country and the plant in which the car was built (B for Britain, G for Germany, then B for Halewood, C for Cologne and A for Saarlouis, although the last is quite rare). The second pair of letters indicate that it's a Capri with a two-door coupé body again, and the third pair, as shown in the chart at the top of this page, the precise month and year in which it was assembled. The vehicle's unique serial number, which follows immediately afterwards, is always a five-digit number between 10001 and 99999.

Moving now to the bottom line of the identification plate, and working from left to right, we come first to 'Lenk' or 'Drive' (note the use of both German and English), and then the 'Motor/Engine' panel, the capacity referring to the basic designed capacity of the cylinder block, not what it might be now. You can work out the meaning of the various permutations from the chart below.

Nominal engine capacity

J — 1300cc
E — 1500cc
L — 1600cc
M — 1700cc
N — 2000cc
Y — 2300cc
U — 2600cc
P — 2800cc
H — 3000cc

Production Figures

1968	3,855
1969	213,979
1970	238,913
1971	211,289
1972	198,875
1973	233,325
1974	183,706
1975	100,050
1976	101,103
1977	91,587
1978	69,112
1979	85,420
1980	41,755
1981	34,658
1982	25,832
1983	27,618
1984	19,508
1985	9,262
1986	10,710
Total	*1,900,557*

Engine type

1	—	In-line, OHV, low compression
2	—	In-line, OHV, high compression
3	—	In-line, OHV, high performance
A	—	In-line, OHC, low compression
C	—	In-line, OHC, high compression
E	—	In-line, OHC, high performance
X/W	—	V4 or V6, OHV, low compression
Y	—	V4 or V6, OHV, high compression
Z	—	V4 or V6, OHV, high performance
V	—	V4 or V6, OHV, medium compression
R	—	V6, OHV, Injection

The next panel, Transmission (ie gearbox), is simple enough. The letter B or the number 5 indicates a four-speed manual gearbox with a remote, floor-mounted shift; the letter D or the number 7 Ford's own three-speed automatic, again with a floor-mounted shift. The five-speed manual gearbox of the 2.8 Injection and the later four-cylinder cars is indicated by the letter F. The nine most commonly used rear-axle ratios and their identifying letters are shown in the following chart.

Transmission

X	— 4.125:1		Z	— 3.54;1
N	— 4.11:1		S	— 3.44:1
C	— 3.89:1		R	— 3.22:1
W	— 3.77:1		L	— 3.09:1
	B	— 3.75:1		

Finally we come to the Colour and Trim panels. Sadly, we don't have the space here to go into the minute detail required for a complete listing of all the possible combinations for all models; but what we can tell you is that in both cases you can glean some useful identifying information from the second of the two characters in each panel. Under Colour you get the last digit of the model year, for example (4 for 1974, 5 for 1975, 6 for 1976 and so on); under Trim you get a rather vague but nonetheless useful indication of the seat-facing material as shown below. The letter Y as the first of the two trim identifying characters indicates it was a special-order colour.

MkII Cars

1	—	Cloth; L, GT, GL
2	—	Cloth; Ghia (Germany)
3	—	Cloth; Ghia (other markets)
A	—	Vinyl; L, GT, GL

MkIII Cars

1	—	Cloth/vinyl
A	—	Vinyl
5	—	Sports trim
Y	—	Special trim

Remember, though, that the model year isn't necessarily the same as the year the car itself was built. The Ford model year always begins when production resumes after the previous year's summer shutdown, so that 1974 model-year cars actually began production in September 1973. Thus the model-year code under the Colour heading won't necessarily be the same as that given by the main vehicle number itself. It might also be worth noting that cars fitted with a vinyl roof at the factory used the second digit of the Colour panel to indicate colour, and THIRD digit to show the model year of the car. So, if your car has a two-character colour code and a vinyl roof, it could just have been added to hide something nasty…

5. Owners' clubs, specialists, books

Owners' Clubs

There are several clubs which deal with the Capri in one form or another. Obvious first choices are the Ford Capri Club International (Field House, Redditch, Worcestershire B98 0AN, tel. 0527 502066) and the Ford Capri Drivers' Association (9 Lyndhurst Road, Coulsdon, Surrey CR5 3HY).

The Ford GT Owners' Club caters, as its name suggests, for go-faster versions of the Cortina, Corsair and Capri (write to Caretaker's Bungalow, Riverside School, Ferry Road, Hullbridge, Essex SS5 6ND), while the Ford AVO Owners' Club and the Ford RS Owners' Club both cover the homologation specials like the RS3100 (and the German RS2600 if you're lucky enough to own one of these rare machines). The AVO Club is at 54 Banners Gate Road, Sutton Coldfield, West Midlands B73 6RU, the RS Owners' Club at PO Box 717, Seaford, East Sussex BN12.

Enthusiasts in Scotland are also catered for by the Capri Ecosse Club which can be contacted at 17 Quayside Street, Leith, Edinburgh EH6 6EJ, tel. 031-553 2331, and there is now even a Ford Capri Enthusiasts' Register. Write to 41 Manningtree Road, South Ruislip, Middlesex HA8 7EG. (All these addresses were believed to be correct at the time of writing but bear in mind that club officials do change from time to time. Several car magazines publish regularly updated club listings.)

Specialists

As for specialists, you could actually do a lot worse than begin with your local Ford dealer. There probably won't be very much in the way of Capri spares ready and waiting on the shelves, but quite a lot of stuff for later cars can still be ordered from the factory.

The Newford Parts Centre in Chorley, Lancs, is worth a try (0254 830343), as is Ludford Parts in Ludlow, Shropshire (0584 875142). Ex-Pressed Steel Panels Ltd of Keighley, West Yorkshire, now remanufactures a useful range of replacement body panels for the MkI, including front inner wings, front lower valances and door hinge pillar repair sections. The phone number is 0535 632721.

Specialised Engines, 15 Curzon Drive, Grays, Essex RM17 6BG, tel. 0375 378606. Suppliers of standard and modified engines and parts for virtually the entire Ford range. Machining facilities and blast-cleaning.

Janspeed Engineering Ltd, Castle Road, Salisbury, Wiltshire SP1 3SQ, tel. 0722 21833. High-performance engine conversion kits.

Jack Knight Developments, Butts Road, Industrial Estate, Woking, Surrey GU21 1JU, tel. 0483 764326. Heavy-duty gearboxes.

Left: By far the largest Capri club in Britain is the extremely enthusiastic and energetic Capri Club International. You'll find their stand at most of the larger classic-car shows, or you can write to the address in the text. (Capri Club International)

Below: As its name suggests, the Club has a truly international following. It organises events in Germany and France, as well as more regular gatherings in Britain, and attracts owners from all over Europe. Preferred styles vary widely, like this Swiss-registered car (left) and the highly modified RS2600 shown on the right. Any Capri or Capri-based special is welcome. (Capri Club International)

Leda Suspension Ltd, Unit 1, Hanningfield Industrial Estate, East Hanningfield, Chelmsford, Essex CM3 5BG, tel. 0245 400668. High-performance suspension kits and parts.

Autocross, Easthamstead Road, Bracknell, Berks, tel. 0344 422220. High-performance suspension kits and parts.

Shaw's Classic RS Components, Unit B, Limes Garage, Eastbourne Road, Blindley Heath, Surrey RH7 6JJ. Tel. 0342 836061. Genuine, reproduction, used parts and panels.

Books

There is no shortage of further reading material for the dedicated Capri enthusiast. Once again this isn't intended to be an exhaustive bibliography, but it certainly lists the major works which are either in print or fairly readily available secondhand.

High-Performance Capri Gold Portfolio, compiled by R M Clarke. Brooklands Books, ISBN 1 870642 988.

The Sporting Fords, Volume 3: Capris, by Jeremy Walton. Motor Racing Publications, ISBN 0 947981 45 4.

Capri: The Development and Competition History of Ford's European GT Car, by Jeremy Walton. G T Foulis, ISBN 0 85429 548 8.

Guide to Purchase and DIY Restoration of the Ford Capri, all models from 1969, by Kim Henson. Haynes, ISBN 0 85429 644 1.

Ford Capri... The Legend Lives. Compiled and published by Capri Club International.

RS: The Faster Fords, by Jeremy Walton. Motor Racing Publications, ISBN 0 947981 21 7. (Covers the complete RS story up to 1987 and contains a useful chapter on RS2600 and RS3100.)

There's plenty of reading-matter for the Capri enthusiast, as this small selection demonstrates. Some of these titles are out of print now, but can often be found at autojumbles, in specialist bookshops or even in charity shops, at easily affordable prices.

V6 Performance; Buick, Ford and Chevy, by Pat Ganahl. S-A Design Books, ISBN 0-931472-13-X. (An American book and thus primarily concerned with Capri engines exported to that country, but covers Cologne V6 in some detail.)

Capri Mild to Wild, edited by Tony Bostock. AGB Specialist Publications Ltd, October 1984. (Another magazine-format publication, this time full of technical information and advice on buying, tuning, restoring and racing.)

Tuning Ford Escorts And Capris. By David Vizard. Speedsport, ISBN 0 85113 090 9.

How To Modify Ford SOHC Engines, by David Vizard. Fountain Press Ltd, ISBN 0 86343 0856.

The RS Fords, by Jeremy Walton. AGB Specialist Publications Ltd. (Magazine-format publication again dealing with whole RS range but again featuring RS Capris.)

Capri International, edited by Tony Bostock. AGB Specialist Publications Ltd, April 1986. (Updated edition of above.)

How To Rebuild Your 1.3, 1.6 & 2.0 OHC Ford, by David Vizard. HP Books, ISBN 0-912656-68-9. (Another book written primarily for the US market, but this time by well-known British tuner David Vizard.)

RS Fords In Colour, edited by Dennis Foy. Windrow & Greene, ISBN 1 872004 71 7. (Extracted from *Performance Ford* magazine and including RS Capri material.)

Magazines

Performance Ford. Published monthly by Performance Ford Ltd, PO Box 14, Hazel Grove, Stockport, Cheshire SK7 6HL. Covers current and recent Fords, including Capri.

Fast Ford. Published monthly by A&S Publishing Co. Ltd, Central House, 154-162 Southgate Street, Gloucester GL1 2EX. Deals mostly with modern high-performance Fords, but runs occasional features on Capris.

6.   Improving the breed

The Ford Capri is a practical, capable and enjoyable means of transport but it is not beyond improvement. And such is the range of accessories, body styling-kits and engine tuning parts still available that you can do as much or as little as you like, or as your budget allows, to tailor the car exactly to your needs.

The limited space available here means we can do little more than point you in the right direction (and we can't get into engine tuning; there are plenty of both general and specific books on the subject); but we'll start with a few words of general advice and what we hope is a timely warning.

The advice is straightforward enough: keep it simple, subtle and, dare we say it, as tasteful as you can. The Capri's reputation for being a sort of automotive Rottweiler is not entirely without justification, and a massive power boost in what may be an already fairly high-performance car without first tackling the steering, suspension and brakes is asking for trouble, if not total disaster.

Likewise, be very careful with body-styling kits. Yes, they can make the car look even better than the million dollars it did to begin with, but again you can come seriously unstuck. Cheap imitations of classics in their own right like the X Pack and Tickford cars (and they do exist) can make even a good Capri look nothing less than a bad joke, and MkI cars in particular can realistically accept no more than a front airdam and/or rear spoiler.

Similarly there's no point in trying to create an RS3100 or Zakspeed lookalike from a car so badly corroded that it will take hundreds of pounds' worth of welding merely to stagger through the next MoT,

or one in such a poor mechanical state that at the first fast bend you come to it will slide off into the scenery. And remember that at some point you'll probably want to sell the car — which may not be easy if you've made radical modifications.

Always start by making sure that the car is structurally and mechanically as sound as you can get it — whatever its specification — and only then thinking about improving first the running gear and then the power unit. And always, but always, tell your insurance company what you intend doing rather than what you have already done. Not only are you legally obliged to inform them of any modifications — no matter how minor — but by discussing your plans first you might also save yourself the embarrassment of finding you can't even afford the inevitable increase in premium.

The first discovery any would-be Capri tuner will make is a fairly significant one and, on the face of it, a disappointing one. Despite its undoubted popularity as a standard road car, and the considerable competition successes it achieved during the 1970s and early 1980s, there's surprisingly little now available off the shelf to improve the Capri's handling and roadholding. Some might argue that that's because they simply don't need improving, but it's more likely that, because the Capri was never in quite the same DIY tuning league as, say, the rear-wheel-drive Escort, relatively few aftermarket manufacturers ever bothered to make the stuff in the first place. Ford itself used to supply a modest but cost-effective range of suspension and brake parts under the Rallye Sport banner, but now they are all but unobtainable new.

John Hill of the Capri Club International runs a 280 fitted with almost the entire range of suspension tuning hardware available from the Club. Here you can see the pair of special single-leaf rear springs and, at the bottom right of the photo, the brackets designed to prevent spring wind-up under fierce acceleration. Note also the aluminium spring lowering blocks just behind the springs, and the disc brake conversion kit with which the car itself has been fitted.

At the front of the same car, John Hill has installed an uprated anti-roll bar and an anti-dive kit (the latter is the piece of box-section steel in the foreground). Also available are uprated springs and strut inserts, of course, along with substantial ventilated brake discs. Even relatively minor modifications, though, can significantly improve the Capri's road behaviour.

That's not to say there's nothing at all available. Ford specialists like Autocross of Bracknell sell most of what you'll need to make the Capri corner and stop in a manner befitting modern traffic conditions, and the ever-enthusiastic Capri Club International offers a good range of hardware, from heavy-duty track-control arm bushes right up to automatic torque-biasing differentials. And, thanks to the car's inherent simplicity, there is also considerable scope for applying to it the standard suspension tweaks which work well on most rear-wheel-drive machines.

The most obvious — and certainly the simplest — way of uprating any sub-2.0-litre car is to equip it with the hardware from a 2.0S or, if it has those bits already, to use the brakes and suspension from a top-of-the-range model like the 3000GT or 2.8 Injection. (If you're thinking of seriously uprating a 2.8- or 3.0-litre car, you'll definitely be into the after-market stuff, but in that case you probably won't need us to tell you what needs to be done.)

Such is the wide interchangeability of parts that virtually any Capri can theoretically be fitted with the mechanical components from any other model, but in practical terms only as sub-assemblies such as front and rear suspension systems (both sides at a time…) or, better still, as a complete set. Bearing in mind that the most likely source of late-model running gear will be an insurance write-off (or a car which has been stolen for just such a purpose), do ensure that the stuff is fit for the job and not likely either to fail under duress or land you in court.

Like any road car where there is a requirement for comfort rather than on-the-limit precision, the Capri has a number of rubber bushes in its steering and suspension systems, and it is possible dramatically to improve the general feel of the car simply by fitting new standard items — particularly if it's one with an unknown history and a lot of hard miles on the clock.

Uprated bushes used to be one of the more popular Rallye Sport lines (they were always cheap, and as simple to fit as the standard parts) but now you'll be lucky to find much more than harder inner and outer bushes for the track-control arms. Steering-rack and front anti-roll bar bushes are well worth replacing, too, particularly if you can find some harder ones, and harder items for the front end of each rear spring used to be a popular move to sharpen up the back end.

For serious competition use you can have bushes made in Nylatron or a similar material to eliminate the slightest trace of unwanted movement in the suspension and steering mounts. These will dramatically increase noise and vibration levels, though, and are *not* for road use. Likewise, the steering and suspension can be fully Rose-jointed if required, but it's doubtful if you would want to replace the joints every 1000 miles or so if you were still using the car on the road.

Moving on to more substantial modifications, an anti-dive kit for the front suspension is a worthwhile investment. The Capri Club's kit consists of a bolt-on box-section which lowers the front mountings of the anti-roll bar by a couple of inches. This reduces nose-diving under heavy braking and minimises changes in the caster angle to give the car a higher degree of lateral stability. Two versions are available: one for all but the 2.8 Injection, and a slightly cheaper one for that model alone which retains the standard roll-bar clamps and rubber mounts.

The steering offers some scope for improvement, too. The first thing you should do, if you have a power-assisted system, is throw it as far away as possible and fit the equivalent manual system. You'll save some engine power and improve the steering response beyond recognition.

Then you can invest in a high-ratio steering rack from the Capri Club. It reduces lock-to-lock turns of the steering wheel from 3.5 to 2.5 and gives a markedly quicker response, but do remember that steering-wheel effort at parking speeds will be substantially increased. The effect is particularly noticeable, of course, with the wider wheels and tyres which are such a popular addition to any Capri — and which we'll cover a little later.

Springs and dampers can make a big difference to the cornering characteristics of any car, and the Capri is no exception. What you must beware of, though, is the temptation to fit the stiffest components you can find in the (mistaken) belief that this will necessarily provide the best handling. What it will do is make the car extremely harsh and uncomfortable — and possibly uncontrollable on all but the smoothest surface.

Bodywise there's a large range of panel kits to choose from even now. Ford itself got in on the act fairly early with its well-known X-Packs for the Mks II and III, and the former in particular (above) still looks a thoroughly purposeful machine. All the panels required to make a MkII X-Pack lookalike are still available from original manufacturers Fibresports, as are those for the Mk III cars (below).
(Photo below, Capri Club International)

That said, there's no harm at all, indeed plenty to be gained, by fitting slightly shorter and stiffer front springs (typically 25mm shorter and 20 per cent stiffer) to reduce the understeer which, because the engine and gearbox are mounted relatively far forwards, can be a problem on any Capri, and particularly the V6-engined cars.

Then, on two-litre cars and below, you can fit the 2.8 Injection's anti-roll bar and, on all models, suitably stiffer adjustable strut inserts (Konis or gas-filled Bilsteins are reckoned to be the best) to keep the whole lot firmly under control. Always

Among the more popular of the after-market body styling kits offered for the Mk III during the 1980s was that from Kat Designs (above and below). It was visually similar to the extremely potent Tickford Capri.

remember, though, that the lighter the engine, the more flexible should be the springs: it's a big mistake to fit springs for the heavy V6-engined cars to the crossflow or Pinto-engined models.

For more serious work you can fit Rose-jointed top strut mountings (basically a spherical metal joint which eliminates the inherent vagueness — and insulation — of the standard rubber component) and even adjustable spring platforms to enable you to fine-tune the ride height and stiffness without large-scale dismantling. Autocross can supply both, and a needle-roller-bearing top strut mount which is more suitable for road use.

A fairly recent development is the Capri Club's two-stage handling kit, developed in conjunction with Harvey Bailey Engineering, a company well known in the tuning industry for its work on Aston Martin, Range Rover and Rolls-Royce. Stage One consists of a pair of ingenious rear-spring clamping brackets which help to prevent spring wind-up (essentially the longitudinal flexing of the spring) but at the same time without unduly affecting spring stiffness.

Stage Two consists of an uprated one-inch diameter front anti-roll bar matched to a 5/8-inch diameter rear anti-roll bar, both bars picking up on the original fixing points on both suspension and body shell. (The kit is compatible only with MkIII cars and can only be fitted to earlier models with the later mounting brackets.) Stage Two, says the Club, can only be fitted after Stage One, and to avoid the possibility of dangerously unbalanced handling both anti-roll bars must be fitted at the same time.

This hardware will make a fairly large hole in your budget, but there are one or two worthwhile tweaks which will cost little more than time and patience. You can, for example, increase the front-wheel camber by about 1/2 to 3/4 degree by slotting the top mounting holes of the front struts until the round-headed section of the rubber-mounting casing touches the inner edge of the large hole in the inner wing. Use large washers to spread the load and, with a proper gauge, set the camber to about 3/4 to 1 degree negative. Finally, set the toe-in (an important but often overlooked aspect of suspension tuning) to about 1/16 inch.

Likewise rear suspension can benefit from de-cent adjustable dampers and modestly stiffer springs. In this case that means installing tapered single-leaf springs — complete with bushes — like those fitted as standard to the 2.8 Injection or, if it's the latter you're modifying, a pair of the improved units sold specifically for that car. In both cases the Capri Club can oblige.

Quite apart from exhibiting a more uniform stress distribution over the whole length of each spring, these lighter units (typically about 22lbs a side) also offer the not inconsiderable benefit of reducing the unsprung weight and keeping the rear wheels more firmly on the ground at all times.

To complement this spring change you can dispense with the standard rubber spacers between the springs and the clamp plates which separate them from the axle casing and, for more precision, again at the expense of comfort and refinement, replace them with similarly shaped aluminium blocks which can also be used to reduce the ride height.

Once again, you must resist the temptation to go overboard on this lowering process, particularly for road use. Even with no load on board the car may be perilously close to the bump stops, and with passengers and their luggage you may find that the handling becomes dangerously unpredictable as the suspension simply runs out of travel.

One thing that is very worthwhile, though, if you have the inclination, skill and/or resources, is the fabrication of a Panhard rod (which fits between the rear axle casing and the body) to give the suspension much better lateral location and significantly improve the car's precision under hard cornering. The rear axle can move over an inch sideways in relation to the body if you really push the car hard.

The ultimate, however, has to be the 'A'-bracket rear-suspension kit marketed by the Capri Club. Designed primarily to uprate 2.8 Injection models to Tickford specification, it consists of a pair of radius arms running forward from the axle casing to the underside of the body and, by triangulating the whole suspension system, it virtually eliminates the lozenging of the geometry under duress.

It's designed as a bolt-on kit which can be fitted in less than an hour (welded-on brackets on the axle casing would necessitate a stripdown to fit them) and that also means, that it can be removed just as

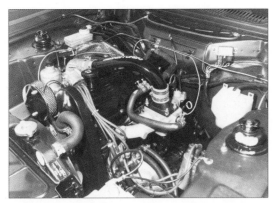

Turbocharging remains one of the simplest and most cost-effective methods of extracting substantially more power from any Capri engine: provided you've tackled suspension and braking modification first, it will provide on-the-road performance you'd scarcely believe. Janspeed offered these two neat conversions for the 2.0-litre Pinto engine (above) and the 2.8-litre fuel-injected V6 (below). Both were designed to be installed with as little disturbance as possible to the engine-bay layout.

easily if you later sell the car. It will fit only the 'D'-type Salisbury rear axle, but is available for either single- or multi-leaf rear springs.

Staying with the rear axle for the moment, consider the value of a limited-slip differential. Like many other tuning goodies, this isn't necessarily as vital as you may have been led to believe (in some cases it can make the vehicle extremely difficult to drive smoothly), but there's no doubt that for seriously fast driving in all weathers that it's a fairly good investment on a high-performance Capri.

The simplest way of acquiring one is to liberate it from the blunt end of a 280, a 2.8 Injection Special, or a 2.8 which has one as part of its optional equipment (but make sure it really is an LSD

before you hand over your cash). Alternatively you could invest in the ingenious Quaife torque-biasing differential marketed by the Capri Club.

Its main advantages are said to be the smooth transfer of torque from the spinning rear wheel to the static one without either the use of the friction clutches in other LSDs or the tendency to make the car run straight on at sharp bends. Unlike the standard Ford limited-slip diff which requires expensive special lubricants, it will also run on standard gear oils.

Saloon-bar racers are usually full of informed-sounding talk about uprated brake linings. 'DS11' and 'VG95' are bandied about like some religious mantra and tend to be seen as the instant cure for all braking problems. Like most motoring myths, this one does contain a grain of truth — races are indeed won on the corners, and the driver who can out-brake the competition does have an advantage — but we are talking here about road driving, where that kind of sustained heavy braking from high speed is rarely necessary.

In fact, heavy-duty brake linings can be a positive disadvantage on the road. High pedal pressures are required (often impossibly high without the assistance of a servo), the linings take ages to warm up and reach their most efficient operating temperature (if they ever do) and, perhaps most significant of all, they tend to glaze over under light loads and become largely useless.

Start your braking improvements, then, by ensuring that the standard system is operating exactly as it should, perhaps fitting a set of intermediate disc pads at the front if the car is to be driven moderately hard. On anything less than a two-litre car, fit that model's front discs and calipers, and spend a little time and money fitting new hydraulic seals throughout the entire system, master cylinder included.

Examine the caliper pistons and their bores for wear or damage and renew any remotely suspect parts (the common Capri problem of a dead, unresponsive brake pedal is usually caused by front caliper pistons sticking in their bores) and fill the system with brand-new fluid from a sealed tin to avoid possible problems of vapour lock. This is a particularly distressing phenomenon caused by water absorbed by the fluid turning into compressible steam at high temperatures and rendering any effort at the pedal virtually useless. Happily it doesn't happen often (although that's more by luck than judgement), but it's far more dangerous and restricting than any limitation of the braking system itself.

Likewise we would caution against the use of silicone brake fluid in all but low-annual-mileage concours-winning cars. Despite its advantages in these circumstances (it doesn't damage paint, and because it doesn't absorb water it will help prevent corrosion inside the hydraulic cylinders), it still boils at a much lower temperature than first-grade mineral fluid straight out of the tin, and it is also very slightly compressible. You'll get a spongey brake pedal, in other words, and that's obviously the last thing you want.

Another trick to improve pedal feel is to replace all the flexible rubber hoses with Aeroquip-type reinforced items — it's surprising how much difference this alone can make — and, to avoid what used to be a common problem on early 3.0-litre cars, to make sure that all the pipe runs are as near the same length as possible to prevent a disconcerting snaking under heavy braking. Reroute the pipes, if necessary, and for long-term safety make up a complete new set of pipes in corrosion-proof tubing like that from Kunifer or Automec.

That should easily cope with most of your braking needs unless you intend to indulge in some very substantial engine tuning. If it still isn't sufficient, though, now you can consider some uprated hardware. Sadly, Ford's own ventilated front-disc kit for Mark ll 1.6- and 2.0-litre cars is no longer available, but you can always used 2.8- or 3.0-litre parts if necessary or, better still, something like the Capri Club's Tar-Ox disc-brake kit.

With 40 grooves machined in each side of each disc, these are said to be tolerant of very high operating temperatures without the usual danger of warping, cracking or fading, and to give a controlled and progressive feel to the pedal. Be warned, though, that they're only suitable for fast road and racing use and will be a waste of money — if not actually dangerous — if the car simply isn't fast enough to warrant their use.

The rear brakes can also be improved by a little judicious parts-swapping — although here again

it's vital not to over-brake the vehicle or you could end up with problems of wheels locking. Apart from the 1300, all Capris have the same rear brakes — which must say something about their efficacy — although the 3.0-litre Essex-engined Capri II and Ghia have wider drums and a working area of 385sq cm while the 2.8 Injection has the same diameter drums but larger shoes and a swept area of 401sq cm.

Further uprating becomes expensive. If you are really serious about going faster and stopping more quickly, the fully floating Atlas rear axle is a must, with or without a limited-slip differential. It can be fitted with a rear disc-brake system by careful selection of parts from AP Racing. It is also possible to convert all 3.0-litre cars built after October 1971 to accept the ventilated front discs from the RS2600 and RS3100, but since these parts and the matching bias-adjustable pedal box are long obsolete from Ford might not be worth the trouble, risk or expense of finding secondhand units.

Last but not least, a couple of minor points which could be of some use. Make sure that the automatic adjusters fitted to the rear brakes of some models function correctly (or perhaps discard them in favour of the more reliable manual type) and, secondly, consider replacing the horizontally mounted rear brake shoes of some cars with the more effective vertically mounted items and their associated double-acting wheel cylinders. To do this you will need all the relevant hardware from a donor car, including the brake backplates.

A carefully chosen set of wheels and tyres can have a tremendously beneficial effect on the way a Capri corners; and a badly chosen set an equally disastrous effect. The first thing to remember is that widest isn't necessarily best. You'll put considerable extra strain on the wheel bearings and suspension, and if the hardware wasn't designed for those stresses then you'll soon be replacing parts left, right and centre.

You'll often encounter problems of tyres touching the bodywork, too, and although these can be solved by a variety of body-styling kits it's not something to be tackled lightly. In general, try to stick to Ford's own wheels — a wide assortment of different and attractive styles have been fitted to the Capri over the years — and remember that, for road use at least, there's little to beat the wheels and tyres fitted to later models like the 280. Another word of warning, though: they are expensive and thoroughly stealable (more on this a little later) and have to be fitted with equally expensive modern tyres to realise their full potential. And those tyres, of course, realistically require to be used in conjunction with suitably updated suspension systems and can also be a lot harsher than their taller, skinnier and more flexible ancestors. You pays your money and takes your choice…

As style objects as well as purely functional ones, wheels lead neatly from mechanical modifications into the equally vast area of body modifications. Inevitably most styling kits are for the MkII and III cars, but there are one or two items available for the MkI. Fibresports, for example, suppliers of all the original X Pack parts for the later hatchback cars, can sell you a set of glassfibre wings with extra-wide Cologne style wheelarches, a front spoiler with air scoops and a 3.0-litre bonnet, and the company also manufactures front and rear spoilers for the RS3100 — ideal if you're trying to create an RS lookalike, or even if you're restoring the real thing.

For the later cars, Fibresports can still offer the full X Pack kit consisting of four wing/wheelarch extensions, a front spoiler with brake cooling ducts, inner rear wheelarches and a petrol filler flap. There is also a Double X kit incorporating most of the foregoing items, plus sill skirts and wraparound bumper mouldings front and rear, and a variety of rear areofoils including a Zakspeed Turbo lookalike, a discreet unit which fits on the roof just above the rear window, and, for the real extrovert, a replica of the Sierra Cosworth-style whale-tail affair.

One of the advantages of the Fibresports panels is that by replacing the standard metalwork with GRP mouldings you can quickly and economically both restyle a tatty Capri and rejuvenate it into the bargain. Fitting involves some cutting back of the original panels, and means that you can't transfer the panels from car to car, but they are cheap enough to be disposable, for want of a better word. Don't forget that with all these kits, and despite our earlier remarks, you may also need wider wheels and tyres to fill the enlarged arches properly.

One of the most popular styling kits from the 1980s was from Kat Designs, and that's still available, too. The full set consists of a nine-panel kit made from hand-laid GRP and, as with other Kat conversions, they are all designed to fit without cutting the original body or the need to bond and/or fill the new material. Thus damaged panels are easily replaced and the whole lot can be relatively easily transferred from car to car. It's intended mainly for MkIII models, but the exterior door panels supplied allow it to be fitted to the MkII which doesn't have the rubber mouldings which normally continue the swage lines of the bumper and wheelarch mouldings.

Rather less ambitious, but no less worthwhile for that, is the Cartel kit. This is designed as a straightforward front and rear bumper replacement exercise, primarily for the MkIII, without encroaching on to the wheelarches, and can again be removed when you sell the car.

Finally, you can create a near-replica (visually, if not mechanically) of the Tickford-converted cars. The five exterior panels — front and rear bumpers/valances, rear spoiler and two sills — are available from the Capri Club International.

From here on, modifications can be as modest or as lavish as your budget allows. Replacement front seats are quite a popular addition in later cars (perhaps with the rest of the trim re-covered to match), and when it comes to electronic gadgetry like stereo systems, power windows and lights the sky really is the limit.

A good alarm system is pretty well essential, given the almost legendary 'stealability' of the Capri, and it might pay to consider some of the other less obvious deterrents. Locking wheelnuts and fuel filler caps are straightforward enough, but consider a set of high-security deadlocks for the doors, a set of shear bolts for the often highly-prized seats in some later cars, and even the old standby of etching the registration or chassis number into every piece of glass on the car.

If you've spent thousands of pounds and hundreds of hours creating the perfect Capri, the last thing you want is some joy-riding hooligan smashing it to pieces, or a professional either stripping it for parts or respraying it and passing it on in some crooked deal.

7. Owners' Views

Such is the breadth of Ford Capri ownership that the only way to capture the essence of what it's really like to own, drive and enjoy one of these fine machines was to talk to a couple of long-term enthusiasts. Dave Sully, for example, has driven his 1983 2.8 Injection for both work and pleasure virtually every day for the last six years, while Andy Smith has spent much the same time restoring his RS3100 to a pitch of perfection which can only be described as exquisite.

The 2.8 Injection was actually Dave's first and, to date, his only car. He bought it in 1985 for £4,700 with the aid of a bank loan, and while it may not have seemed a particularly sensible choice to his friends and family at the time, his cost per mile since then is more than compensation for the soul-searching he went through before taking delivery.

'I knew all about the perils of buying a car like this from a young chap like the previous owner,' he says now with a shrug, 'and I'm sure that this one had been in a fairly major shunt, if the repairs to one of the front wings are anything to judge by. But in the event, it's been a fantastic car.

'The idea was to get something reasonably fast which I would enjoy driving, but which at the same time I could service and repair myself if necessary. It had 24,000 miles on the clock, and I thought I might take it up to about 80,000 or so in the three years I initially planned to keep the car, so the fact that it's still going strong today really is a bonus!'

Indeed, apart from obvious costs like fuel and road fund licence, Dave's major expenditures have been on insurance and consumables like filters, brake pads and spark plugs.

'I knew that it would be expensive to insure, of course,' he smiles. 'My first year's premium — fully comprehensive, mind you — was £400, and over the years that's only come down to about £300 as my increasing no-claims discount has been eroded by inflation. But what else can you expect for a Group 8 car?'

Dave has never regretted his choice from a driving point of view, either. 'I was very taken at the time by the Escort XR3,' he admits, 'and I enjoy driving a friend's RS Turbo, but I really wanted something a bit bigger and a bit more, well, exclusive. I wasn't over-keen on the original Capri, either, but I tried one of these later models and found it really very nice to drive.

'There was obviously lots of power there, but it always felt safe and, by giving a lot of warning if it was about to come unstuck, it was actually a very forgiving sort of car. And I still find it extraordinarily comfortable, even over long distances. I drove it to Berlin and back when the wall came down and enjoyed every minute of the trip.'

Mechanical problems have been refreshingly few and far between. The car needed a new steering rack fairly early on in Dave's tenancy — although he's still not convinced that the garage which failed it on the MoT wasn't simply making a fast buck out of him — and it's had two water pumps. But with 140,000 miles on the odometer now it's probably entitled to them.

'I think the original pump probably wore out prematurely because that same garage over-tightened the belt,' he says, 'and after that I always tried to do the more major overhaul work myself,

Dave Sully's 1983 2.8 Injection has covered over 140,000 miles and is still going strong with no sign of impending mechanical disasters — although the bodywork is beginning to look a little frayed round the edges. Dave attributes its reliability both to careful maintenance and the rectifying of any minor problems as they occur... and the basic strength and reliability of the design.

as well as the basic servicing.

'Engine-wise it still seems perfect. It always starts first time, summer or winter, as long as the battery is up to scratch — I'm on about the third, I think — and I've never even touched the fuel-injection system. I've adjusted the tappets once or twice when they've become noisy, but apart from that I leave the motor to get on with it.

'I've always used genuine Ford parts,' Dave continues, 'you know, filters, belts, that kind of thing, and I've changed the engine oil and filter every 6000 miles without fail, and I'm convinced that's one of the reasons it's been so reliable. The only problem I've ever had with the engine itself was a misfire after I'd renewed the plugs on one occasion, but even that was my fault for reconnecting the leads incorrectly!'

More recently, Dave has fitted new front brake discs, wheel bearings and anti-roll bar bushes to tighten up the front end in readiness for an MoT test ('the bushes were a pig to fit,' he says) and not long before this was written he'd finally tracked down what he had originally thought was a worn-out final drive to nothing more serious than time-expired rear wheel bearings.

'For ages I'd had this annoying rumbling through the whole car,' he says, 'and I'd convinced myself the rear axle was falling apart, but in the end I put it right about £20. There's still a slight resonance through the car at about 55mph, but that could be the centre bearing on the propshaft. I'll investigate that when I've got time!'

Sadly, though, Dave's Capri is now beginning to look its age. He's the first to admit that he's not lavished any particular cosmetic care on it, but he was understandably disappointed when the door pillars began to erupt with corrosion in the typical Capri fashion.

'I can understand things like the front wings going rusty,' he says, 'and the rust in the tailgate was my own fault for backing into something, but the rot in the "A" posts was pretty ghastly. I've patched it up as best I can with glassfibre mat, and it looks reasonable now, but I'd look very hard indeed in that area if I was ever thinking of buying another one.'

Not that it seems particularly likely. Still Dave says he'll keep his first and only Capri until something major goes wrong with it, and still it keeps on keeping on.

'It's part laziness, I suppose, and part unwillingness to spend a lot of money on a car which is probably little better than this one in so many respects, but I really can't see any reason to sell it,' says Dave. 'I can't see it getting to the stage where it starts costing me a lot of money to repair — if the engine blew up tomorrow I know I could get another one from a dismantler — and I still love the shape, so what's the point?'

Andy Smith acquired his RS3100 in much the same condition that Dave Sully's 2.8 Injection is in now and, like him, initially used the car for nothing more than interesting everyday transport. But there the resemblance begins and ends.

'As a genuine RS3100 it was always a little bit more than just another tatty old Capri,' says Andy, 'but even I didn't fully appreciate its historical significance at the time.'

Andy used the car for his daily 60-mile round trip to work and back for about six months before having the engine fully rebuilt and performance-tuned, and the body resprayed; then he carried on using the Capri for another year until, in November 1987, it was involved in a substantial pile-up.

'I was waiting to turn right at some traffic lights,' he recalls, 'when some idiot jumped the lights and smashed into the passenger's side.' Perhaps not surprisingly, Andy's insurance company decided the car was economically unrepairable and wrote it off. 'It needed two doors,' continues Andy, 'inner and outer sills on both sides, inner and outer rear quarter panels on both sides, inner and outer rear wheelarches on both sides and an outer wheelarch on the other. It was a real mess!'

Eventually, though, a deal was struck. The car had been valued at £5,000 before the accident, so the insurance company paid out half that and gave Andy the wreckage. 'I was pretty upset at the time,' he says, 'but I soon realised it would be a marvellous opportunity to rebuild the car to the standard I'd always wanted but never really had the incentive to start.'

Sensibly, Andy didn't lay a spanner on the wreck until he'd found most of the panelwork he knew he'd need to finish the job. 'I sat down at work with a list of UK Ford dealers,' he laughs, 'and simply

Andy Smith rebuilt his RS3100 from the ground up after it was involved in a serious road-traffic accident. As exemplified by the view of the engine compartment, it's near-perfect in every detail — and certainly the ideal car to be featured on this book's front cover.

rang as many as I could to see if any of them had old-stock Capri or RS panels on their shelves. It wasn't amazingly successful, but I did get most of what I wanted in the end.'

The next step was to get the body shell restored to its former health. Realising his limitations in this field, Andy farmed the work out to a local body-shop where, in the event, the Capri was to spend the next two years. Andy says it was well worth the wait, though.

'They made a superb job of it. I'd hoped to have the car back on the road for summer 1990, but obviously they couldn't do all the work at once, and in any case I was quite happy for them to fit it in round other jobs if it kept the overall cost down.

'I used to take the day off now and then and go there myself to do some of the donkey work, but even so the total bill came to just over £6,000. Mind you, that included everything — repairs, stripping, paintwork, the lot.'

While all this was going on, Andy busied himself with the running gear which he'd kept in storage at home. All the suspension parts were sand-blasted and painted before being reassembled with new nuts and bolts, then when the body was finally finished he took all the hardware to the bodyshop to get the shell mobile again so he could tow it to another workshop for the engine to be fitted.

By his own admission, Andy had gone 'a bit mad' with the engine the first time round, but now he decided that originality was more important — so off came the Weber 40DFI carburettor, the Bosch vacuumless distributor and Janspeed exhaust manifolds, and back went the original parts which he'd had the foresight to keep.

'I renewed just about every other mechanical part I possibly could, though,' confesses Andy. 'Bearings, bushes, pipes and hoses, alternator, starter, all that kind of thing. I bought a pair of new Bilstein rear shock absorbers, the braking system is new from front to back — oh, and the gearbox was rebuilt with all new bearings.'

But all that, reckons Andy, was probably the easy bit. What really gave him a problem was finding the badges, brackets, trim and mechanical parts unique to the RS.

'I needed a rear spoiler, for example,' he says, 'and in the end I had to take the one off the second RS I'd bought to use as daily transport while this one was off the road. It provided the RS spoked wheels, too.

'Mind you, not having the right spoiler was my own fault. The car had the right one on it when I bought it, but thinking it looked a bit tacky and not realising its significance, I simply threw it away! I learned my lesson, though, and after that kept literally everything that came off it, no matter how small. You can't be too careful with this historical angle, can you?'

The Capri is nonetheless a remarkably convinc-

ing example of the breed. Andy is continually searching for more small parts to recapture the way it looked when it left the Halewood factory in November 1973, and reports with justifiable satisfaction his discovery of the correct air-filter casing in a fellow enthusiast's garage, along with a bonnet stay, now bright cadmium-plated exactly as it should be.

'The trouble is that you just don't see MkI Capris in scrapyards these days,' he says, 'never mind three-litres, and certainly never an RS. There are probably only four or five RS3100s as good as this in the country,' he continues, 'and the sad fact is that there will almost certainly never be any more. Some of the more obvious cosmetic parts are now being remanufactured on a small scale — decals, badges, carpets, that sort of thing — but the really important stuff, from body panels to trim clips, is impossible to find.'

Andy relates how he had to buy a 1972 GT to get a lot of the minor hardware he needed for his own rebuild. 'It was a shame to have to break up a car which was certainly not beyond repair and, in its own way, probably just as significant as the RS3100, but it was the only way I could think of to find everything I needed.'

He admits, too, that even now the RS isn't really finished. The interior, while not too badly worn for a vehicle this age, was simply thrown back in again to get the car mobile, and Andy has plans for a full refit in the near future. He wants to reposition some of the under-bonnet brake pipes. There's still a reversing light switch to fit to the gearbox. And even the brand-new battery is earmarked for replacement if ever Andy can find the Ford type installed when the car was new.

'I'm looking for a set of front number-plate brackets,' he laughs. 'I'm told they're the same as the ones used on a MkII Cortina, but I can't even find one of those in a scrapyard which has still got the wretched things!'